THE SOUTH AND THE NORTH IN AMERICAN RELIGION

THE SOUTH
AND THE NORTH
IN AMERICAN
RELIGION

Samuel S. Hill, Jr.

Mercer University
Lamar Memorial Lectures
No. 23

THE UNIVERSITY OF GEORGIA PRESS
Athens

Set in 11 on 13 pt. Linotype Baskerville
Printed in the United States of America

Library of Congress Cataloging in Publication Data

Hill, Samuel S
   The South and the North in American religion.

   (Mercer University Lamar memorial lectures; no.
23)
   Includes index.
   1. Christianity—United States—Addresses, essays,
lectures. I. Title. II. Series: Mercer University,
Macon, Ga. Lamar memorial lectures; no. 23.

BR515.H54   277.3   80-234
           ISBN 0-8203-0516-2

Contents

Foreword

WHEN MRS. EUGENIA DOROTHY BLOUNT LAMAR ESTABLISHED
the Lamar Memorial Lectures in 1955 her wish was to aid
the preservation of southern culture, history, and literature.
In the first twenty-two lectures delivered under the provi-
sions of Mrs. Lamar's will, the admonition has been met for
the most part by lectures dealing with politics and literary
criticism. The present volume, however, departs from this
established format by focusing upon one of the most
powerful forces in southern life that has not yet been ex-
plored in these lectures—the southern church.

The Lamar Memorial Lectures Committee had for many
years been committed to bringing to the Mercer campus a
specialist in southern church history and religion. This commitment led ultimately to Dr. Samuel S. Hill, Jr., as the
twenty-third Lamar lecturer, a choice substantiated by impressive credentials and an established reputation. Professor Hill's academic preparation includes a degree from
Southern Baptist Theological Seminary and the doctorate
in religion from Duke University. He has served as chairman of the departments of religion at the University of
North Carolina and the University of Florida; he is now a
professor at the latter institution. His important scholarly
publications include *Southern Churches in Crisis* (1967)
and *Religion and the Solid South* (1972). Not least in this
catalog of accreditation is the fact that Professor Hill comes
from a family that has played an important role in southern

religious life, his father having been president of George-
town College (Kentucky) for a number of years.

The lectures in this volume were delivered in abbrevi-
ated form on the Mercer University Macon campus on 29–
30 October 1979. The enthusiastic and responsive audiences
appreciated the quality of Professor Hill's lectures, the clar-
ity of his style and delivery, and his ability to combine
rigorous intellectual standards with his own personal involvement with his subject. The comparative methods that
he employed stimulated much interest in and a further
understanding of the complex and largely unexplored
world of southern religious life and experience. Mercer
University is honored to present these lectures to the American public.

Henry Y. Warnock, Chairman
Lamar Memorial Lectures Committee

Mercer University
Macon, Georgia

Preface

IT IS FITTING THAT THE LAMAR LECTURESHIP SHOULD FOCUS attention on the religious dimensions of southern history and culture. For a century and a half, and more, the American South has been permeated by the Christian religion and dominated by one family of that massive tradition, evangelical Protestantism. To this day, notwithstanding the winds of secularization, naturalism, and positivism, its people remain attached to the church and responsive to religious teachings, perhaps more so than anywhere else in Christendom. Examination of southern religion has been made timely by the prominence of Evangelicalism (and related movements) in American society at large, beginning with the late 1960s and the election in 1976 of a president whose speech and behavior reflect this kind of orientation.

The field has begun to receive extensive and increasingly mature scrutiny in recent years. From the publication of Kenneth K. Bailey's *Southern White Protestantism in the Twentieth Century* in 1964 to recent books by Donald G. Mathews, E. Brooks Holifield, and Albert J. Raboteau the work has been going on, and much more is underway. The subject is so vast and specialized, however, that several decades will be required before its treatment can catch up with the advanced state of scholarship in the political, literary, economic, historical, and other dimensions of life in the region. And, given a new vision and boldness, concerning the unity of life in human society, the study of religion may take on unusual importance, inasmuch as both method and substance are inherently interdisciplinary.

I can only hope that this group of lectures will contribute
to the enlarging, ripening field and advance the state of the
art. One reviewer of recent studies of religion in the South
regrets the absence of a standard authority and an authoritative text. She writes perceptively: "Without a classic work
which investigates, illuminates, and takes a stand on various issues (no matter how controversial), one is left casting
about in a chaotic universe with no Archimedian point."
That need exists. This book does not satisfy it; if anything,
it underscores the urgency of the accomplishment she calls
for. Yet it may be another tributary making its contribution to the larger stream, inasmuch as it seeks to transcend
any period of southern history, any denomination, either
major race of people, and indeed the South itself.

Many people have noted that comprehensive study of
religion in the South is overdue. C. Vann Woodward wrote
in 1952 that "national histories of religion for the most part
deal with tendencies conspicuously lacking in the South."
Martin E. Marty, in a note on a recent publication which
treats the South in the American Revolution, expressed a
wish "that the authors had done a comparative north-south
study of religious involvements." Marty's concern reminds
us that "comprehensive" really means national; southern
patterns have needed investigation badly, but they should
not be treated without significant reference to the national
framework.

By now anyone taking up this topic has a number of mentors and colleagues. In southern religious history, one thinks
of Kenneth Bailey, Hunter Dickinson Farish, Ernest Trice
Thompson, Rufus B. Spain, John L. Eighmy, Donald Mathews, John B. Boles, H. Shelton Smith, Brooks Holifield,
Albert Raboteau, Walter B. Posey, and David E. Harrell,
Jr. In comparative north-south studies my debts are greatest
to C. Vann Woodward, John Hope Franklin, Carl N. Degler, Paul H. Buck, Clement Eaton, and Fletcher M. Green
—the last two of whom aided the cause through their lec-

tures in this series. In my own case, indebtedness to and
agreement with Degler are the most substantial. We both
emphasize that the South is not a monolith, that it nevertheless portrays an "overall unity that embraces the diversity,"
and that it is different from the rest of the nation—Degler
terms this difference a "limited distinctiveness." ×

Sydney E. Ahlstrom's *A Religious History of the American People* (1972) moved to correct the deficiencies in southern religious historiography that Woodward lamented. It
achieves very high standards indeed in scanning the entire
American panorama, incorporating regions, periods, races,
organizations, and points of view. From a different perspective, I have already sought to think comprehensively in
several published pieces. That different angle is a sociological angle of vision on historical developments; it has
produced analysis more specifically comparative than comprehensive. I believe that way of addressing the topic is in
line with the stated purposes of the Lamar Lectures, since
comparison of religion in the South with religion in the
North holds promise for illuminating southern religion,
culture, and history in its distinctiveness.

Thereby hangs the tale. This is a cross-cultural American
analysis; it explores two cultures *within* the same culture,
which in many respects are the same culture. It is this curious state of affairs which suggests the utility of a comparative, in other words, a more sociologically inclined approach,
in addition to the fruits yielded by more strictly historical
methods.

I intend for this to be very much a historical study, even
though it is not carried on in the historian's manner. Joseph
R. Gusfield's description of his methodology in *Symbolic
Crusade* characterizes my own here: "This book is an interpretation rather than a history because our interest is largely
with the analysis of what is already known of the movement than with the presentation of new data." Such a venture is not without risks. Aware of the dangers involved, I

have looked for key issues within southern society and culture as compared with northern, and selected analytic devices for interpreting them.

"Cross-cultural American" analysis? What a strange jux-
taposition. One is bound to conjecture whether there are
analogues in modern western states. Do Wales and Scotland
within the United Kingdom qualify? Does the Basque culture within Spain? Or the various states in the Soviet Union?
Or Austria-Hungary before World War I? The American
condition of cultures-within-culture is hardly unique, yet it
is laden with curiosities. With reference to the religious dimensions of American culture alone, we observe that between South and North: (a) the denominations are the
same; (b) the people of the mainstream groups, as to ethnic
stock and cultural tradition, were the same for 250 years or
so; (c) the two regions have lived under one government for
all but four years; (d) the theological traditions are basically
the same. It is tempting to wax sentimental (and excessive)
in an exclamation like "Secession, the Civil War, and the
formation of the Confederate States of America were
impossible!" Far more useful because far more true is the
straightforward observation that southern distinctiveness, in
religion and all other aspects, is filled with curiosities. We
will examine some of those in the pages which follow.

Five goals, all of them finally melded, characterize the
efforts undertaken here. I am seeking to describe the religious situation in each region during three crucial epochs,
the dominant events and types of development in each, relations between the two regions, relations between the religious life of the regions, the relation of religion to regional
culture in each region. As hinted at earlier, a sixth (indirect)
goal is contemporary and something of a composite of these
five: to sort out Evangelicalism in America today by way of
helping various groups of Americans understand each other
through seeing whence they came and how they have come
to be as they are. To accomplish these goals I will need to

give attention to the religions themselves—to theology, systems of belief, the essence of particular religious traditions, and the phenomenology of Christianity. So, this is not just a book about religious history viewed from a sociological perspective; it is also about religion and the logic and dynamics of belief.

A full treatment of what a "religious situation" is cannot be pursued here. But several of the ingredients in the religious situation of any period will be evident in the chapters that follow, including: (a) what continues as usual; (b) what the new features are; (c) what the tensions are; (d) what the social issues and problems are that call out for attention; (e) what extremism looks like; (f) who the heroes or representative figures are; (g) what opportunities and resources are available to religious organizations; (h) what the relation between religion and the belief of the unchurched is.

The choice of 1795–1810 as Epoch A, 1835–1850 as Epoch B, and 1885–1900 as Epoch C was partly arbitrary. Yet in another sense, given the limitations of scope delineated by this lectureship, these selections were obvious candidates and deemed compelling. It was essential to reflect on critical periods in southern history, but no less basic to identify formative eras in the North beyond. Obviously, any two had to be congruent to qualify; in the final analysis, a period was determined on the basis of its being epoch-making for the South. With the same principle of protocol in mind, fuller treatment is provided for the situation in the South than in the North.

Many observers of American society have noted our tendency to dualize and hyphenate, no one better than Woodward in his book with the suggestive title, *American Counterpoint.* He reminds us that we are fond of structuring relations in society contrapuntally, to wit, East-West, North-South, White-Red, White-Black, Old Settler–Immigrant, Protestant-Catholic, Gentile-Jewish, and so on. Focusing on details, he notes such anomalies as the "southern ethic in a Puritan world," "Protestant slavery in a Catholic world," and "southern slaves in the world of Thomas Malthus." However, one senses that he is as anxious as I am to bring to an end any contrapuntal thinking which issues in ill will, divisiveness, or claims to superiority at another's expense. He writes: "North and South have served as inexhaustible objects of invidious comparison in the old game of regional polemics. *Our* faults are as nothing . . . compared with *theirs*." One hopes that the destructive qualities associated with the polemical dialogues of the past may have been laid to rest forever. The facts of their reality, ofttimes painful for many decades, however, is the provocation of this study. It is hoped that the translation of that fact as fact to perspective for inquiry may illuminate southern culture and history.

The decision to undertake this study resulted from an invitation extended to me by the Lamar Memorial Lectures Committee to deliver the twenty-third set in that series. I did so at Mercer University on 29–30 October 1979. My gratitude for their invitation is best registered by my acknowledgment that that is the finest professional honor I have received. I was deeply gratified by being asked to participate. My respect for the series was deepened by the thoughtful and gracious hospitality accorded my wife Claire and me. We will always be grateful to the members of the Committee, the Departments of Religion and History especially, a number of other individuals, and, most of all, to Professor Henry Y. Warnock who orchestrated all the activities. It was such a pleasure to be treated as "really somebody" by people from the Mercer University and Macon communities that I fervently hope this book will enhance the stature of that campus and the Lamar Lectureship.

Samuel S. Hill, Jr.

Gainesville, Florida
January 1980

Introduction

THE CAREER OF RELIGION IN THE UNITED STATES OF AMERI-
ca has been singular when compared with its place in other
modern western nations. That is a datum known in advance
by everyone who has considered the matter since the entire
American experience has been uniquely its own. Less well
known is the nature of the singularity in the area of religion.
In the final analysis the American disestablishment of religion and the adoption of the principle of voluntarism are
the qualities which have set off our nation's religious life
from that of comparable societies.

All of the other societies of Europe and Latin America,
probably without an exception, have inherited the traits of
an establishmentarian philosophy; either one church has
been the society's tradition and enjoyed governmental support and sanction, or the understanding of religion's role in
that way has left its legacy. From the formation of the Republic, disestablishment, the guarantee of religious liberty,
diversity, and, quite recently, pluralism have characterized
religion's place. Practice has not always accorded with theory, needless to say; eternal vigilance is required in this
aspect of American life as in all others. Jews face this problem more persistently than any other Americans, but Roman
Catholicism, Protestant sects, cults, and today's "new religions" have had their brushes with it too. Nevertheless, the
theory has been quite generally supported and its implementation increasingly realized, with the result that its con-

sequences are felt throughout, by all classes and sectors of the society. One wonders if there is anyone left who seriously wishes for a pattern of establishment; even the most radical, sectarian, and exclusivist religious groups acknowledge the right of other groups to coexist, even though they may deem them false and perverse.

The South's version of this theory with its history has been peculiar within the larger pattern of singularity. It goes without saying that the law of the land has pertained to Dixie as much as any other area. But the specific points of contact between theory and practice have differed according to the ways in which the religious and demographic history of the South have been peculiar. The Roman Catholic population has been small and its real "threat" minimal; the Jewish population has been far smaller and the presence of Jews no real issue. Cults and "new religions" have been sparse. Sectarianism had been tolerated for nearly a century. On the other hand, homogeneity and claims to regional purity have made for some snobbish attitudes, resulting variously in infrequent violence against dissenters and, often, a less-than-accepting "Why can't you be like us?" spirit.

So there have been differences between South and North in the relation of religion to society. On one level, the most important has been the persistence of the supposition that "this is Protestant country," or at least a fervent wish that that were so, for a century longer in the South than in the North. At another and deeper level, the divergence has been determined not by time but by outlook. Specifically, the Christianity of the North has regularly declared its responsibility for the health and direction of the society at large, while the church in the South has not. Since this fact in its complexity (the relation of religion to its regional context) comes close to being the most fundamental aspect of southern religious history, it calls for clarification and elaboration. In these processes, however, we must remember that the South is seen truly for what it is only in a national framework, that is, in comparison with the North.

Christianity in all of its classical expressions has had three basic components: theology, piety, and ethical responsibility. *Theology* refers to its conviction that it lives by truth, a truth which must be believed, continually reexamined, and promulgated. *Piety* refers to religious experience, the awareness by the people of the reality and presence of God, something which must be nourished and heightened. It is expressed in personal devotional life and in the public celebration of ritual action. *Ethical responsibility* refers to appropriate conduct and action, to personal righteousness and moral duty to others. Roman Catholic Christianity had acknowledged this componential structure of the faith for centuries before the appearance of Protestantism. The Calvinist party in that school of interpretation recast a great deal but conserved that fundamental three-dimensional understanding of the Christian faith. It was this Calvinist formulation of the faith that informed the minds and souls of most colonial American Christians. Without question, New England was Calvinist in outlook. The kind of Anglicanism which planted religion in the southern colonies had much Calvinist sentiment in it as well. And the progenitors of Evangelicalism in the South lived under the influence of Calvinism to a greater or lesser degree. Moreover, Wesleyan (Methodist) versions of Christianity acknowledged and stressed the place of all three components.

More directly to the point, the New Englanders dreamed of magnifying the "ethical responsibility" component of the faith to the stage where their society would be a holy commonwealth, a theocracy, the manifestation of a purified, authentic Christian civilization. They set about putting dreams into action. For several decades they created virtually what they wanted, in form at least. Truth to tell, they were so successful that they helped elevate interest in the corporate, the public, the societal—in a word, the political —to the point where secularly political concerns displaced their explicitly Christian-based goals for the common weal. Despite this secularization, however, the mainstream of Christianity in the North retained its basic conviction that Christianity has much to do with the common life, with "Christ as the transformer of culture," with public and social ministries which were to be carried on in behalf of people's lives and contexts irrespective of their religious affiliations. We see this most dramatically in the extensive social reforms wrought during the generation before the Civil War, the Social Gospel movement which flourished between 1890 and 1920, and, noteworthy in our own day, the intense social concerns of several parties of northern Evangelicalism. The centrality of ethical responsibility in northern Protestantism especially is highlighted by the relatively minor (or perhaps derivative) place given to "piety," except in the groups outside the mainstream, a fact which in itself helps make the point.

It has been otherwise in the South, but the difference is complex, subtle, and ironic. A close, formal continuation of England's establishmentarianism was the intention of the colonists in Virginia, Maryland, the two Carolinas, and Georgia. Those societies were not designed to be holy commonwealths as such, but a Christian civilization no less, in the manner of Christendom. Lewis Simpson's researches into colonial southern literature show that in contrast to the New England settlers' image of their errand into a wilderness, Southerners viewed their new habitat as a paradise. Theirs was an "errand into an open, prelapsarian, self-yielding paradise, where they would be made regenerate by entering into a redemptive relationship with a new and abounding earth."[1] In searching for the religious sources of such an outlook, one realizes how much affinity it has with establishmentarianism within Christendom and, to boot, with Anglicanism. This is the language of stability and gradualism, of the affirmation of the world pretty much as it is. In Richard Niebuhr's classic typology of the five ways in which "Christ" and "culture" are correlated, this is the "Christ *of* culture" pattern, very different from New England's radical conviction of "Christ the transformer of culture."[2] The Southerners' domicile was His domain, in the nature of the case, as the establishment of England's church in this, its societal extension in a grid of parishes, amply attests. This arrangement presupposed the baptism, thus Christian identity, of all citizens. Conditions and circumstances were to militate against the realization of that conservative dream, however, so that "working at" Christianizing the population became the rhythm of the southern church, much later, of course. In the North, the earlier approach of "working at" evangelization gave way to a more indirect and casual rhythm, which was to prove statistically less successful in the long run.

In their disparate ways then, and with diverging careers once the colonial era had come to an end, South and North began with basically Christian visions for society—for moral society as well as for moral individuals. The traditional European notion of the ontic distinction between (and inconfusability of) society and persons survived the long passage across the Atlantic.

Leaving aside consideration of origins now, we should note a salient feature of the career of religion in America: the nature of American society has forced religious issues into the open. They have made up a sizeable proportion of the legal and social concerns which have been affecting Americans and America during our history. Religion has been a rather public affair here, demanding the resolution of issues in a way quite different from that prevailing in societies where one church was established. In the absence of a single-church pattern, or one normative tradition, religion has been intrusive and its role a bumpy one. It has been forced to make its own way in a society prizing voluntarism. It has also been subject to many organizations and diverse interpretations; the consequence of this has sometimes been competition between groups, sometimes a need for protection from the tyranny of the majority, and often the demand on each group to share its favored position with others despite the group's felt superiority. The indomitability of religion and religious organizations in the face of myriad problems reveals the strength of the venture and the responsiveness of the American people to a religious understanding of reality. "No state church" has meant anything but "no church at all."

To say that American society has forced religious issues into the open, or made them public business, means that ethos (Greek for "context" or "setting") has been vitally important. Obviously, *ethics* is an English derivative from the same root, referring to conduct in the public arena. American religion has been centered on ethos, but ethos in two senses: alertness to the context in terms of which the institutional life of religion is framed; and ethical responsibility to the ethos, other people as individuals, and society (and lately to the physical environment). Thus, in addition to the obvious fact that the churches have acknowledged a social responsibility, they have had to take special note of their societal and cultural contexts in order to be relevant. Their roles in and relation to the larger setting not being defined in advance, as in established church societies or even quasi-Christian societies, they have been forced to adapt, adjust, map strategies, and engage that setting as it is. After all, in America religious organizations can go out of business. Thus *relevant* is a strong term reflecting certain necessities that have been imposed on religious institutions here. Those have been successful which have been vitally connected with the sensibilities and needs of real people. Of course much of this "engaging" and "connecting" has been unintended—this phenomenon has been variously called the unconscious functions of religion, the unintentionality of history, the inadvertent by-products of religion. Simply stated, religion in America has been ethos-concerned both *for* society—responsibility—and *to* society—responsiveness to conditions in the context.

Some kind of ironic quality in southern history has been widely noted owing to the "incongruities between moral purpose and pragmatic result," in Woodward's classic words on the subject. I believe we may also observe a more specified irony of southern *religious* history issuing from this discussion of ethos. We may term it "ethos without ethic." A religious tradition which has not been much concerned with social ethics (and was often apolitical) has been attentive to, sometimes preoccupied with, its ethos or context or setting. The church in the South has not seen responsibility for the society as its primary task, yet it has been inordinately responsive to its societal-cultural framework. Also, as a great deal of recent research into the history of religion in the South has demonstrated, the evangelical tradition implanted a sense of order and community, and a moral basis for a viable societal existence. Whether these were stated goals of the churches or not, they were their significant contributions. Donald Mathews shows how profound Evangelicalism's *social* impact was in this observation: "Religion became identified with an essential public reaffirmation of social solidarity. Going to church became not merely a religious act, but a civic responsibility."[3] What he notes as prevalent in the Old South is only slightly less true today.

In the lectures themselves, we will examine how and why the dominant tradition happened to escape formulating a social ethic. But we will also be seeing how often something like a social ethic actually emerged; the most dramatic instances are the churches' support of slavery in the antebellum period and their vigorous leadership of antialcohol crusades late in the nineteenth century. In both cases, they were responding to conditions which were testing and straining the society, rather than generating policies, *ab initio,* out of their own theological context. Some denominations have sometimes managed to stay clear of and remain untainted by concern for such worldly matters, but they are mostly of later origin and are markedly outside the mainstream. The popular churches have been too much a part of the society to find it possible to maintain a sectlike stance relative to it. Often intending to limit themselves to spiritual matters, they have been deeply involved in the secular affairs of southern society just the same. Intending to be prophetic, to brandish a sharp edge in criticizing an imperfect world they yearned to redeem, they have often been captive to that culture's values and perspectives.

A large part of the story to be told here through a comparative regional analysis has to do with the essence or dynamic of religious belief-systems themselves. The supposition is that religion has some kind of "independent variable" status, that is, that it is a force in its own right. In other words, what southern Evangelicals have believed about God, people, and the world on the basis of the Bible's teaching has been a contributing factor to their behavior. With specific reference to the "ethos without ethic" theme, their theology has helped determine the ranking of the three components, piety, theology, and ethical responsibility. By all odds, piety has stood in first place. The salvation of individual souls and the cultivation of an inner sense of the divine presence have outstripped all other goals and achievements. Right belief, while hardly absent, has been recessive and functional; theological definition and elaboration have not been a hallmark of the southern enterprise. Ethical responsibility has been a highly selective concern, as earlier intimated, being strongest in the area of personal conduct. How different things have been in the North, despite the denominational and theological (and other) similarities already referred to.

As we compare, two devices will be used. The first is expressed in the pair "near" and "far," and treats the question of interaction between South and North. In the three epochs surveyed, 1795–1810 (Epoch A), 1835–1850 (Epoch B), and 1885–1900 (Epoch C), what was the state and degree of actual relations between the two regions? Were people in touch; corresponding; involved in common enterprises; traveling back and forth in business, pleasure travel, for educational purposes, and the like? Was commerce active between the two regions? The second device is expressed as "close" and "distant," and refers to the cultural similarity and harmony or their opposites between the two regions. Does each take for granted the other's membership in the same national society? Is there respect by each toward the other? To what degree do they see eye-to-eye and cooperate on significant issues? Is there a fundamental agreement on what is valuable and what the desired nature of American society is? Are they traveling in the same direction on parallel tracks, or not? "Near-far" and "close-distant" are used to help ascertain the relations between South and North along empirical and attitudinal lines, respectively.

It may be apparent from such a contrapuntal or comparative approach that I begin with the judgment that the South has been a distinctive society and culture (within limits) and has had an identifiable unity notwithstanding its considerable diversity. A second inference is just as basic, namely, that South and North are two regions of the same nation, the same society, and the same culture. There would not be either one if there were not the two in one. It is their divergence within an indisseverable unity which creates the historical experience being recounted here. Rhys Isaac has made the generic point very well in this axiom: "Opposites are intimately linked not only by the societal context in which they occur but also by the very antagonism that orients them to each other." Not even the severe strains of the nineteenth century could drive a lasting wedge between the two regions, despite the South's tortured decision to opt for local honor rather than national unity when the irrepressible conflict came.

As far as religion, or more properly theology, is concerned, South and North have had distinctive careers inside the pervasive unity of a Protestant Christianity that is dominantly Calvinist. Northern society began with a theological essence that bulked large for the mentality and social policy of the entire society. It was clearly an English Puritan version of Calvinism. Moreover, it was carefully formulated and richly elaborated through the erudite labors of New England and old world theologians, Dutch as well as English and Genevan. It was a "complete" interpretation of Christian meaning in that all three components, theology, piety, and ethical responsibility, came in for thorough treatment and extensive application. I conclude that it is possible to rank them according to theoretical importance or practical functioning in colonial New England life, so comprehensive was their vision of a holy commonwealth on American soil. That was a solid beginning indeed; a theological essence and comprehensive social program were sustained by a seriousness of concern to build a new and pure colony of heaven on earth.

Its subsequent history has been complicated to the point of being many histories, not one. Very broadly speaking, it has passed through these stages: dynamic efforts to recover the original essence in the Great Awakening; the rivaling of a theocratic design by the rise of political preoccupation; a lengthy series of adjustments, reinterpretations, and accommodations in the face of a plethora of new outlooks in the natural and social sciences and historical and humanistic

studies; religious diversity, then religious pluralism, and finally rampant ideological pluralism with secularism in the
vanguard.

By contrast, the religion of the South began without a
pervasive style; its form of Christianity probably was most
effective in the area of "ethical responsibility." But that was
understood in a very special way, as permeating the ethos
with the civilizing and stabilizing influence of Christianity.
Subsequent history has consisted in: planting an essence,
which was the mission of the two Awakenings; spreading
that essence to pervasiveness; accommodating religion to
emerging regional conditions; linking religion and region;
strengthening the regional religious institutions and spreading their message at home and abroad. Summarizing in
terms of our three-component form of analysis, the North
began with a strong theological tradition, with piety as its
life-force and social responsibility as its mission. The chal-
lenges to it have been dominantly of an ideological (or theological) sort. The South began with an Anglican notion of
ethical responsibility, but piety displaced it and made it a
religious society and the kind of religious society it has been.

There is little difference between South and North on
the question of relatedness to surrounding society and culture. Whatever intentions and claims, each has been at
home in its setting. If at any time it did not find itself in a
societally compatible posture, it adjusted accordingly. Such
is the lot of religious institutions in the world, to one degree
or another. Nevertheless, distinctions between developments in the two regions are dramatic, ranging from origins
to historical developments, to particular responses and
adaptations.

Tracing these distinctions diachronically through three
specific historical periods is the essential task of this book.
In the South of Epoch A, the religious situation was fluid,
unpredictable, flexible, premature, actually preformed. It

still smacked of a European character, though increasingly under conditions which were not hospitable to that interpretation. Concurrently in the North, the situation was changing and mobile owing to new social conditions, but at the same time given direction because it was anchored in the concrete original vision of the Puritan founders.

As for Epoch B, terms such as regularized, routinized, and normative, set and expanding, without rival or dissent, fixed and defensive, apply to the southern situation. The briefest inventory of northern traits highlights the disparity: diverse, accommodating, and modifying. During Epoch C at century's end, the South's religious situation was set and exclusive, and religion was all-dominating. The northern situation could hardly be more different; divided, pluralized, and amorphous are terms which come to mind. Accommodating new climates of opinion and assimilating new imports had become standard practice, eroding the old base from which strategies and responses were made. In point of fact, the "new climates of opinion" and "new imports" were fast joining the traditional religion as fellow keystones in the religious situation.

ONE

First Cousins Separated
1795–1810

THE WAR FOR AMERICAN INDEPENDENCE AND THE FORMA-
tion of the United States of America altered American society and at the same time left a great deal intact. Without
a doubt, this dualistic single event marked the dramatic
emergence of a new era for Americans, and in truth, for the
rest of the world as well. However, at the level of everyday
existence, much went on as it had been going for the past
several decades.

A glance at the relation of the society and culture of the
people south and southwest of Maryland around 1800 reflects both of these features, the newness of things and a real
continuity with life as it had been. As for continuity, southern people remained apart from their northern fellow coun-
trymen in point of actual contact and in socioeconomic style.
"Apart" is largely accurate, but we must be clear that
"apart" or "separated" are facts which are byproducts of
circumstance rather than attitudes of aloofness or antagonism. Distance and difficulty of transportation largely confined Southerners within their own geographical territory.
It is true that commercial interaction between South and
North was considerable, and began to increase after Whit-
ney's invention of the gin made cotton king. Yet "apart"
does describe the real situation during these earliest years
of the new nation. South and North penetrated each other
relatively little. There is scarcely a word in John Hope

Franklin's study of the interaction, *A Southern Odyssey*, about the years before 1820. Real interaction did characterize the antebellum period, but during 1820–1860 for the greatest part. There was no necessity, nor attraction, nor time for Southerners to think or travel northward; the same held true, for different reasons, for people from the North concerning the South. As a matter of fact, both were traveling, but westward; not infrequently they jointly settled in some trans-Appalachian locale.

It is important to underscore the sharp contrast between "apart" or "separated," conditions which prevailed in this period, and "alienated" or "divided," terms which characterize Epoch B of our study, 1835–1850; likewise with Epoch C, 1885–1900, where "strangers in the same household" is an apt phrase. Unlike the later periods, Epoch A displayed no basic enmity or sense of antagonism. Geographical and socioeconomic circumstances distinguished the southern territory and people from those of the North, but that was the extent and true nature of the relation. It was "far" rather than "near" with reference to distance and vigorous interaction, yet also "close" rather than "distant" from the standpoint of attitudes and cultural unity. Neither enmity nor alienation, not even aloofness, accompanied apartness and separation at this early stage in the history of relations between the two regions of the new Republic. As Charles Sydnor and Carl Degler have pointed out, the South participated vitally in the development of democratic political institutions in the early republican years, also in the social reform movements of the period, and led the nation in the development of public higher education.[1] The South was very much a part of things and in step with general American trends.

Yet the seeds of those kinds of attitudes were being sown before the turn of the nineteenth century. This is seen clearly in the discontinuity between the colonial and early national periods. At the same time, we must remember how closely connected are the continuity and the discontinuity, the two being little more than sides of the same coin. The major new development being pointed to is the coming into being of a sense of southern identity, and soon, solidarity or unity. While this regional self-consciousness did not harden or crystallize until after 1830, it had made its appearance by 1800. And how different this was from the conditions prevailing in the colonial period, when there was no South as such. There were people who lived in the southern colonies, a simple geographical referent, but there were no Southerners so designated by themselves or by others. Degler concludes that the South was an idea, but not much more than that by 1789. His research has disclosed "a sense of difference rather than a deeply felt or perceived distinction or identification."[2]

This was due in part to a considerable disparity of topography and people, as manifested in the three or four different modes of existence in the southern colonies to which Carl Bridenbaugh calls attention. Most prominent was the Chesapeake Society, comprising the people, values, and occupations of the Virginians and Marylanders on either side of the Bay and stretching inland as far as the rivers were navigable. Here tobacco was the principal crop. Also rather settled was the Carolina society, chiefly the lowlands from Wilmington to near Savannah, where the growing of rice and indigo shaped economic and social life. Behind these stabler and more civilized societies was the Back Country, where hunting and mixed farming occupied the labors of the people. Bridenbaugh conjectures that a fourth mode may have been operative in seaboard North Carolina where there was a small population and neither primary crop nor well-settled communities.[3]

A South, then, there was not—nor Southerners, as late as the date of American independence. Yet there were two

common qualities which prefigured the South: the presence
of Negroes, with their special and fixed roles in the society,
and a rural way of life. These two, of course, were inter-
twined. Negroes as slave laborers were required to sustain
an economy founded on the civilization of cash crops. We
begin to see how this previous discontinuity gave way to an
interregional connectedness in the debates which took place
over the status of slaves and the degree of their citizenship as
the Constitution was being hammered out. We may also
note this inexorable drift toward strong regional identity
in the attitudes shown and decisions made by the most
X prominent religious body, the Methodist church, from its
organization in 1784, on the subjects of slaveholding and
membership by slaves. From a restrictive policy on members' ownership of slaves through a number of gradual compromises, to a position of silence on ownership, the first nine
or ten Methodist General Conferences seriatim made their
peace with the prevailing economic and social conditions of
the culture. Paradoxically, as the church relaxed its stands
on that issue, it stepped up its efforts to convert Negroes to
and instruct them in the ways of Christianity. Donald Mathews summarizes this evolution as a movement from a concern to emancipate to a vigorous program of evangelization,
with a number of stages intervening.

The most conspicuous traits of the religious situation in
the South from 1795 to 1810 were fluidity and unpredictability. During these years the never-too-illustrious career
of the colonial religious establishment, the Church of England, reached its nadir, not to rise again for half a century.
This is not to say that the established church was powerless,
however. For example, it retained certain privileges and
rights for itself, such as performing marriage ceremonies
and the insistence that all school teachers hold membership
in it. But by the 1760s dissenters outnumbered churchmen
in every southern colony. From the perspective of respect-

ability and tradition, religion was careening off the preci-
pice. Wise, history-minded citizens must have lamented the
end of an era which, although far from glorious, at least had
roots in the past and promised direction into the future.

In the place vacated by the established church some
strange new sects were taking over. There had been Congregationalists, Quakers, and Presbyterians before 1700, it is
true. Yet these had made little general impact because they
were not given to aggressive tactics, a trait based on their
envisioning their responsibilities as largely limited to the
respective immigrant peoples who had planted them in the
region. Traditional Baptists were living along the South
Carolina coast from the 1690s onward, but they too were
more parishlike than evangelistic in their styles of ministry.

In the 1740s, around Richmond, the southern phase of
the Great Awakening erupted, thanks at first to Presbyterian
leadership. But the real beneficiaries and indeed promoters
of this new movement of the divine spirit were to be the
Separate Baptists who appeared from 1755 and, in the latest
phase, the Methodists whose radical version of Anglicanism
swept over the Virginia countryside beginning in the late
1760s. The Presbyterians were in the picture, even in some
revivalistic forms, but their role was far less flashy—or prom-
ising—than that of the Methodists and the Baptists. Thus,
by the last decade of the century, some things were clear but
others were cloudy. The Episcopal church (organized as
such in 1785) would not be established or effectively planted in the southern states. The Presbyterian church would
be present and a force to reckon with; yet how vigorous a
force would it be? Could the Methodists and Baptists com-
mand enough depth and stability to continue to give their
zeal direction? Could churches like those be the dominant
forms of Christianity in a postestablishmentarian society?
Fluidity and unpredictability were indeed the ranking facts
of the southern religious situation in 1795.

It is worth noting that developments in the Church of England helped break the soil from which the evangelical churches could spring forth. For a few decades before formal disestablishment, such democratic practices as vestry power and home rule had become common. Accordingly, in some measure disestablishment only recognized attitudes and policies which already existed. Perhaps the democratization of the church and the phenomenon of the evangelical denominations sprang from the same soil, rather than the former helping prepare the way for the latter.

Here is another instance of a discontinuity between the colonial and early national periods which is more apparent than real. The evolution metaphor comes closer to capturing the actual situation. Nevertheless, we must not overlook the sharp struggle which was occurring between the Anglicans and the Baptists just before the Revolution. Rhys Isaac has shown that much conflict and persecution attended the "radical social revolt" conducted and symbolized by the "Baptist style." These people from the classes below the gentry opposed and rejected traditional mores and in the process created a new "social world."[4]

We have alluded to the presence of Negro slaves and intimated that these inhabitants of the South played a part in the religious situation. But the actual facts of southern society require moving beyond allusion and intimation toward explicit acknowledgment of the formative role of Negroes in the religious life of the South. By 1795 their population numbered about three-quarters of a million; of these some 3 percent were church members, mostly in the Methodist and Baptist denominations. The conventional wisdom of twentieth-century American whites usually has it that black people are incurably religious and always have been; in other words, that the slaves were Christianized rather easily, quickly, and thoroughly. Not so.

The story of the Christianization of the Afro-Americans

who were brought here from 1619 onward is a lengthy and complex one. In order to set the backdrop for our examination of the period 1795–1810 and the two subsequent epochs, at least an outline must be presented. The white churches and people were reluctant and half-hearted in the efforts they did make to instruct the Negroes in Christianity. For their part, Negroes responded infrequently. At the beginning of the national period hundreds of thousands of the heathen were marking out their existence in the midst of a Euro-American civilization for which there was no real religious alternative to Christianity. More than a little concern had been demonstrated on behalf of their induction into and instruction in the faith, but it was sporadic. Albert Raboteau characterizes the religious situation among Afro-Americans in the colonial period this way:

Only a small minority of slaves received instruction in Christian faith. The objections of slaveholders; the unsettled state of religion in the southern colonies, which held the great majority of the slave population; the paucity of missionaries to catechize slaves; linguistic and cultural barriers between Africans and Europeans; the very way in which conversion was generally perceived—as catechesis, a time-consuming process of religious instruction—all these factors ensured that Christianity touched most slaves indirectly if at all. There were, however, a few slaves who did accept Christianity and were baptized into the Church under Anglican, Puritan, Baptist, Quaker, and Moravian (a very few) auspices. Some attained full if not equal communion with their white fellow Christians.[5]

It will not do, however, to leave the impression that the Afro-Americans were unaffected by the prevailing religious context, either because they retained traditional African religion more or less intact or because they cast off any religious perspective. Raboteau suggests two reasons for which "Africans became New Negroes," that is, were significantly affected by the religious instruction given them by whites. The first is the number of relative similarities between

Protestant Christianity and African religious belief. Thus, the slaves were able to "find some common ground between the belief of their ancestors and those of the white Christians." One example is the connection between the Christian doctrine of the trinity and the African religious teachings about a plurality of divinities. Two others are belief in an afterlife and the central place accorded adoration and prayer. On these and related grounds Raboteau reaches a different conclusion from those who have theorized that the slaves were adopting a totally alien worldview when they embraced Christianity.[6]

The second impact made upon the slaves by the religion that only a few of them actually accepted had to do with its establishing a kind of rhythm of life which later, under the impetus of the conversion experience, would make sense. "The complete cycle of a sacramental progression from baptism to burial, with the special training of each successive step between, including the learning of the white man's language, might not be a legal emancipation, but was, nevertheless, a participation in the white man's folk ways, amounting to something like tribal adoption."[7]

At the dawning of our Epoch A, there were also a few Jews, situated almost exclusively in Charleston, Savannah, and Richmond; a Roman Catholic population, sizeable where it existed at all, in Maryland, Mobile, and Louisiana, but otherwise nominal; a smattering of Anabaptist descendants in the valley of Virginia; and some German Protestants in the Piedmont section of the two Carolinas.

But, to repeat, the situation was fluid and unpredictable. With the benefit of hindsight we can see that the patterns of growth, were there to be any at all, would belong to those denominations that belonged to no special social group, neither an ethnic community nor an economic class cluster and which were therefore in a position to be aggressive rather than stable and typed. The Methodists and the Baptists were these groups. These were the churches of the masses, people who had held little before the Revolution and therefore lost little when the new society was born, and who in fact played the role of midwife in the birth. It was they with their relentless missionary zeal and infectious enthusiasm who were to turn a religiously fluid condition into a Methodist-Baptist, evangelical-revivalist society and culture. And this was as true of their impact on the black population as of their successes among the white. So far, what we have said about the South has referred to the original, the South of the seaboard colonies, from Maryland down the coast to Spanish territory at the Georgia-Florida boundary. But from the 1780s on, the South had a trans-Appalachian dimension as well (a point to be made concerning the North, too, in this same period, as we will see presently). This new feature of American society would make enormous impact on the nation's life between 1820 and 1860 when decisions had to be made concerning whether newly admitted states from this "West" were to be slave or free. But in the short run too, and with specific reference to organized religion, the opening of the western territory was destined to exercise heavy influence on southern society.

In 1799, 1800, and 1801, the Second Great Awakening broke out in Tennessee and Kentucky. Not that it was called that by any of the participants, most of whom recalled little of the First, even its southern manifestation of 1745–1770, and certainly not that it had much in common with the far more conservative Great Awakening of New England in the 1730s and 1740s. But, though somewhat novel, it was a powerful religious and social force, a true awakening, and even, according to William McLoughlin, one of the major periodic revitalizations of our culture. This was the real beginning of "frontier religion" or "folk religion" and of the camp meeting phenomenon. In time the camp meeting generated revivalism, to this day the most popular means for converting lost souls in the religious life of the South. Parallel to earlier outbursts of vital religion, this frontier occurence was guided by Methodists and Baptists, with Presbyterians sometimes in a supporting role or even occasionally as instigators. Because this frontier religion was so formative a force in its own time and continues in modified forms as a major manifestation of southern religion until today, its anatomy as a belief-system calls for treatment in some detail. Its basic premises are: the exclusive authority of the Bible for revealing the nature and will of God and the responsibilities of his human creatures; the fundamental duality of reality, the being of the personal God viewed as morally perfect and requiring, over against each individual person regarded as morally defective and deficient; the person of Jesus Christ, God's only son, who died on the cross to make payment for the sins of every person; and the freedom and responsibility of every person to repent and decide to follow Christ. This version of evangelical Protestantism— there were variations on the theme then and there are other varieties now—was, to begin with, very sure of its position and very active in promulgating its message. Seen this way, the Christian meaning and task are urgent matters. Every person is lost, without God, without hope, the way, or the truth, and must be told the news. This news is bad news before it is good news, but it is all of a single piece. Christianity thus interpreted is a problem-solution system. Those who are devout will spotlight the tragic flaw in all and the deliberate transgressions of each, hoping thereby to rescue the perishing from a desperate, eternal condemnation to hell. They are exhorted and pleaded with to receive the pardon of their sins, which is realized by accepting God's salvation, offered to them through the merits provided by Christ's atoning death. When the condemned sinner repents and opens his heart to receive saving grace, he is born again; that is the experience of conversion. From now on he lives in sweet and close relationship to the Lord and, especially, with the glorious assurance of everlasting life beyond death.

Religion so conceived can be programmed. The terms are clear, the goal is spelled out, the incentive is keen. Accordingly, techniques fit. Two such took shape under western frontier conditions, the camp meeting and the protracted meeting or revival. One suspects that these frontier conditions had much to do with the acceptability of revivalist-style Evangelicalism with its two techniques. There was a large population to be won to Christianity, with rare and brief occasions for accomplishing this crucial occurrence. Both camp meeting and revival sought to achieve the same goals, the conversion of lost souls, but their approaches differed slightly. In the former the people came to a designated place and camped for a few days. Preaching, singing, and testifying went on pretty well around the clock, under the trees or brush arbor and around a rough-hewn platform or specially carved stumps. Protracted meetings—revivals, they came to be called—occurred in a church building, with services being held once or more a day over a period of several days or even two or three weeks. Both methods of accomplishing the Lord's work relied on the transcendent work of the Spirit. But both also fell into stylized ways of presenting the message, softening and encouraging the hardhearted, and bringing people across the line that separated life from spiritual death. In other words, there developed an orthodoxy of means to accompany orthodoxy of belief.

What really mattered was the experience, the moment when one was delivered the assurance that he or she had been pardoned of sin, restored to fellowship with the Lord, empowered to walk in godly ways, and promised everlasting life. The conversion experience as a form is seen most clearly in contrast to what it replaced, the traditional Anglican route to making Christians, namely, religious instruction. As Raboteau puts it:

Evangelicals were as concerned as Anglicans about observing the rules of Christian conduct after conversion, but it was the *experience* of conviction, repentance, and regeneration which occupied the attention of the former. While the Anglican clergyman tended to be didactic and moralistic, the Methodist or Baptist exhorter visualized and personalized the drama of sin and salvation, of damnation and election. The Anglican usually taught the slaves [and any others coming into the church] the Ten Commandments, the Apostles' Creed and the Lord's Prayer; the revivalist preacher helped them to feel the weight of sin, to imagine the threats of hell, and to accept Christ as their only Savior.[8]

That these techniques were successful is borne out dramatically by the statistics of membership growth; the number of white Methodists increased from some 38,000 in 1792 to 46,000 in 1801, to 80,000 in 1807. While southern blacks were not yet being enlisted in large numbers, they were beginning to come into the fold, and Baptists and Presbyterians also were marking up impressive gains. The fact of success would also seem to be supported by the intense nature of the experience being felt by thousands. Donald Mathews tells us that "great numbers of people were affected by strange seizures of uncontrollable weeping, fainting, groaning, and barking. Evangelicals had witnessed such spectacular phenomena before, but never in such magnitude."[9] He is making reference to the modulation, among the earlier English Wesleyans, Southerners and New Englanders, of demonstrations of the Spirit into a higher key, and on a broader scale, among the people of Kentucky and Tennessee between 1799 and 1810.

Since we are looking at things longitudinally, we must again highlight the persistence of revivalism and the forms of Evangelicalism with which it is associated in order to register adequately the degree of the success of this frontier religion. At the conclusion of the decade of the 1970s conversion-oriented evangelical Protestantism holds on as the standard regional recruitment approach, with the Southern Baptists, much the largest denomination, deeply committed to this as the task God has called them to and the means he has provided. Other groups too make this the highest priority. For those who do not interpret Christian meaning and responsibility along these lines or recruit new members in this fashion, this popular view occasions problems inasmuch as it is widely regarded in the culture as the measure by which Christianity is to be judged.

To the considerable extent that the essence of Christianity was viewed as the conversion of individuals, reality was reduced to two constituent units, God and the individual. In actuality the picture was seen as larger than that, as we are about to observe. But one significant side-effect of this simplicity was what it did to theology and theological activity. Theology was brought down to earth and stripped of complexity. All an individual or a congregation needed to know was what the Lord requires and prescribes for personal salvation. That was far from nothing, to be sure; doctrines of biblical authority, the Trinity, Christology, salvation, church, regeneration, human free will, justification, and sanctification, among others, amount to a considerable list. Sermons took note of them and class instruction pointed them out. Yet this catalogue of Christian teachings was simple and functional in that every item in it served the purpose of personal salvation. That was the pivot of all the doctrines; the one vital doctrine was a teaching about experience, not something requiring the exercise of the intellect or an act of assent. In a manner of speaking, we may then say that the theology of this kind of Evangelicalism, which gradually became the dominating interpretation throughout the South, militated against the theological training of both ministers and lay people. They knew and taught what they knew and taught; mostly they were determined to know only "Christ and Him crucified." It follows that they devoted little attention to any searching examination of even the tenets they prized. In this view Christianity identifies, in some sense creates, the existential problem crying out for the divine solution. Evangelistic preaching is intended to create a spiritual crisis by calling to the fore one's desperate and lost condition, which one may have been totally unaware of. Understood this way, Christianity does not seek to link basic human questions with answers, nor to provide assertions which then raise questions. This is self-styled "simple Christianity," in more ways than one. Accordingly, Methodist and Baptist preachers received the benefits of limited education, the latter especially. The Presbyterians gradually excused themselves from revivalistic Evangelicalism, partly because of their tradition's roots in a more comprehensive view of truth, sophisticated doctrine, and rational thought, which in turn entailed education for ministers (and was deemed desirable for lay people as well). As we shall have opportunity to observe in the subsequent chapters, there seems to be something of a positive correlation between a conversionist orientation to Christianity and the fundamental dispensability of serious education, especially of anything resembling the classical sort.

The prevailing theology did reduce reality to two constituent units, God and the individual. Yet the necessity of elaborating Christian meaning, plus people's having to come to terms with everyday life, stretched Christianity's application beyond that trim anatomy. For one thing, education did become important later, in functional ways especially. For a second, Evangelicalism transcended its own declared individualism inasmuch as the very execution of its program of conversion implied building a fellowship which one shared with others and taking responsibility for other people. Beyond any question, it engendered a sense of community. McLoughlin reminds us that the Second Awakening "stressed localized unity . . . a sense of community. Camp meetings were communal in nature; churches became the centers of community life; and, above all, although a conversion was an individual confrontation of the soul with God, the sustaining fellowship of Christian brethren provided the continuity that routinized and canalized the fervor of the awakening into orderly social institutions." [10] In continuing he notes concrete ways in which this kind of religion brought order to the community: "by restraining violence, strengthening self-discipline, and encouraging familial and neighborly responsibilities for good behavior."

Mathews extends the point farther by arguing that "community" and "individual" did not constitute a polarity among these southern Evangelicals. For, he writes, both values were present in their experience: "Intense introspection, subjectivism, and voluntarism" on the one side; on the other, the initiation of the individual "into a permanent, intimate relationship with other people who shared the same experience and views of the meaning of life and who were committed to the goal of converting the rest of society." [11]

In a comparable public or communal, yet distinctive, development, Evangelicalism had earlier played a role in breaking down the social class hierarchy the southern colonies had inherited from English society. Mathews makes the point very well in describing the common people and religion's usefulness to them:

They were independent folk who had been successful enough to resent the invidiousness of the distinction between them and the aristocracy, but humble enough to take certain stubborn pride in the inadequacy of traditional social distinctions to define them. They were moving not only through space (to better farms) and time (to a better status) but also through eternity, that is, to a community which replaced the traditional ethic with a new one. Whichever aspect of movement one emphasizes, these people were moving away from old social ties to new ones. . . . [There is evidence] that Evangelicalism attracted people who were dissatisfied with conventional society. . . .

Evangelicalism therefore was a means through which a rising "new" class sought authentication outside the archaic social hierarchy. . . . They were trying to replace class distinction based on wealth and status—they called it worldly honor—with nonclass distinctions based on ideological and moral purity. . . . Whatever name we give to this process . . . it produced a new social reality.[12]

We can observe this transcending of theological individuals in a couple of other ways and by doing so further establish the degree of religion's role in the formation of southern society. It is important to see that this entire discussion is meant at the phenomenal level to show how significant organized religion, its congregations, doctrines, and ministers were in the shaping of southern life. At a subtler level, the role of religion was, if anything, more powerful. It added much impetus to and provided legitimation for the emerging regional self-consciousness. Let us recall that three decades or so earlier there had been no South and no Southerners. By 1800, however, forces had been set in motion which transformed the term from geographical reference to social and cultural meaning (and incipiently, political and legal, as well). Religion in part fostered this emerging spirit, partly set a stamp of approval on it, and partly provided organizing mechanisms for the accomplishment of it. It is impossible to put a finger on precisely what religion contributed; but its place was a large and fundamental one. It is somewhat easier to see the outcome of this melange of forces driving toward a new social condition: The South came into being as formulated, coherent culture, politically aware, distinctive in its own eyes and before others.

But that is to move a bit beyond the actual occurrences

of Epoch A. All we have reason to speak of at this juncture is that southern people were even more religious than they knew themselves to be, that the South was more religious than its number of churches and believers gave indication of. In a phrase, when the South got religion, it opened itself to a powerful, sometimes ungovernable force. The novel religious patterns and approaches, being intense, aggressive, geared to success, and demonstrably genuine made spiritual reality larger than life. This led to the uncontainability of the power generated by religious awareness. It swept out in directions unintended and unacknowledged, becoming a vibrant force in arenas for which the converted assumed no formal religious responsibility: specifically, culture, society, secular values, "natural law," and eventually politics. In the course of this evolution, the South became not only identifiable, distinctive, and self-aware, it was also on its way toward regarding itself as pure (purer than the North at any rate) and superior. The flowering of these attitudes into values and policies came later, but the seed is in Epoch A.

For elaboration and illustration we turn once again to McLoughlin:

Commenting on the intense concern with personal morality in southern religion, John Boles has written, "If anything, pietistic revivalism on the individual level decreased concern with politics." Christianizing the social order in the South, as among the more intense holiness groups in the North, meant converting every individual to the basic moral pattern of rural middle-class virtue. The awakening challenged southern culture—or was allowed to—only in terms of private self-control. In a land with little real poverty, no urban slums or factory towns, minimal cultural conflict with Roman Catholic immigrants, with the Indians moved to the West and the blacks considered childlike beneficiaries of civilization, the white southerner felt that his region of the nation was already closer to millennial perfection than any other part of the country. Was not the South a region of farmers, and had not Jefferson said that the farmer was "nature's nobleman" and that the republic was safe in his hands? As the camp meetings and new churches Christianized the southern frontiersmen, and stabilized their rough habits, the South's celestial railroad seemed further along its track to the kingdom of God than any of the celestial railroads in the North.

In the North, the Second Great Awakening challenged the older way of life at every turn, producing endless schisms and theological debates. In the South, after some initial denominational turmoil in the first decade of the century, this awakening confirmed the prevalent life-style, increased religious homogeneity, and made the Baptists and the Methodists so dominant that other sects were an almost invisible minority. Southern white Christians were not averse to benevolent reform if that meant encouraging personal temperance and helping the orphan or widow, the deaf, the dumb, the blind, the insane. But if it meant rearranging the social order, tampering with slavery, interfering with state sovereignty, defending the Indians' right to remain on good farm and cotton land, then benevolent reform was totally misguided. It was in fact, un-Christian, since it created political tests for spiritual organizations. Whether a man held slaves or not was irrelevant to his right to join a church.[13]

The dynamic of religion could not be confined to its formal channels such as doctrinal and moral teachings; it burst those banks. But it also was walled off from penetrating the societal structures which were reflections of traditional values. This was due both to the formal fact that these matters were considered to lie outside the churches' responsibility and to the depth of the validity claimed for these conventions, which no voice from the society was at liberty to broach. Let us be clear that there is no justification for a totally cynical view of the churches' performance in this respect, to the effect that they had no perspective or courage since they were bound in cultural captivity. It is true that they had (and have had) little leverage on their relation to the regional culture. But it is just as true that their ideology made no place for or encouragement toward involvement in political, economic, and legal structures. Thus, southern

Evangelicalism taught and practiced a personal ethic which, while larger than (and an addition to) an individualist ethic, was smaller than a social ethic. It also embedded itself in the ethos of the society by inculcating values, attitudes, and definitions of the good life which came to be taken for granted and were rarely thought of as associated with or legitimated by religious teaching.

In sum, between 1795 and 1810 the role of religion came to be powerful and dominant. This had to do with both the intended goals of the churches and with its adventitious insinuation of values and modes into the lives of all people, the unchurched as well as the churched, black as well as white.

A final mark of religion's affinity to the culture is seen through the indigenous Christian movements which appeared in this era. This point is merely a particularized instance of a general principle widely applicable to understanding religion in American culture, namely, that the birth of new (usually rather strange) versions of Christianity on American soil reveals a great deal about the nature of the society at the time. In the South, two of the four strands of the Christians or Disciples of Christ movement (organized in 1830) appeared during Epoch A. These were the O'Kellyites, fathered in 1794 by James O'Kelly, a Methodist minister in Virginia and North Carolina; and the Stoneites of 1802, who were led by Presbyterian Barton W. Stone of Kentucky. A third innovation came with the emergence of the Cumberland Presbyterian denomination in western Tennessee and Kentucky around 1808. While the two "Christian" ventures and the Cumberlands did not take off from the same starting-blocks, they did envision a comparable finish-line. All wanted to throw off hierarchical organization in favor of—those magic American words—freedom, liberty, republicanism. O'Kelly was fed up with the "ecclesiastical monarchy" in the Methodist church of which he had been a stalwart leader. Stone was obliged to renounce Presbyterian church organization toward his goal of being merely Christian and according authority only to the New Testament. Both of these pioneer spirits also had had their fill of formal theology, preferring instead only what the Scriptures teach. Any good Methodist, Calvinist, or Baptist would of course have said the same thing. But O'Kelly and Stone exchanged concepts for texts, creeds for verses, a complex whole for undifferentiated parts, and reflection for subscription and practice.

Finis Ewing and the Cumberland Presbyterians were less concerned with organizational matters than with the relation between doctrine and piety. For them the accomplishments of the camp meetings and revivals demonstrated the truest character of religion, vital piety, the direct experience of the Lord in one's heart. The theologically inclined Presbyterian tradition thus needed reform. Failing to get their way in bringing that about, these frontiersmen pulled out to form their own presbyteries.

Differences among these three there were. Yet they held some convictions and tastes in common. Furthermore, they were to be the last indigenous Christian emergents (except for the Wesleyan Methodists of the 1830s) until late in the century, when the Holiness movement erupted, a point not to be taken lightly. All three were for the "common man" or "plain folks," wanted to replace religious hierarchy with congregational, even individual, rule, and distrusted theology, whether as learned thinking or as mode of knowledge, preferring the interpretations or experience of the people. Clearly, these stirrings reflected the work of the heady wine of liberty, the enthronement of republican virtues. A new social order had come into being; religion must and did take its place in that *ordo novum seclorum* as surely as politics and law.[14]

These indigenous developments demonstrate that the

South was laced with irony, paradox, and unpredictability in the early years of the nineteenth century. It was as liberty-infected as the rest of the country. At the same time it was a geographical territory becoming a region with ideological consensus, having its distinctive styles and values, soon to be defended by attacks on other liberty-loving Americans. Southerners were indeed first cousins to their northern fellow-countrymen. If they did not interact with them profusely in this period, they did literally belong to the same stock ethnically, and figuratively speaking they belonged politically. A major irony is visible from this period forward in that the southern whites turned their fondness for local church government into an opportunity for making regional, even local, decisions about the welfare of slaves. Having only loose connections with national or other extensive jurisdictional authority, they plied their own course in line with regional conventions. Further, magnifying the religious experience in the heart of the individual as they did, they could conclude that slaves were being treated justly, even compassionately, through their sharing of the gospel with them. Religion, by such means as these, became all of the following: incentive to render life's most valuable service, making Christians, to the slaves; a confirmation of the non-evil and legitimate character of slavery as an institution; the cement of southern society; the occasion for localist understanding of the nature of society.

How different things were in the northern states at this time, and yet how similar and interrelated. Comparing the two religious situations, we may differentiate the northern from the southern, which was earlier described as fluid and flexible, by means of terms like *changing* and *mobile*. The South's being "fluid" suggests the absence of a normative tradition; a centripetal force had been developing there for a generation or two, but its power was not yet harnessed. The dominant positions were still pretty much up for grabs.

In the North, a truly effective establishment of religion had prevailed from the era of beginnings, the 1620s. Congregationalism had been the publicly sanctioned and subsidized church in all of the New England colonies—except Rhode Island, which was thought the worse of for that neglect. Moreover, it had been as powerful and formative as it had been prevalent. If the South was an extension of Christendom by hope and an outpost of English life in fact, the North was a kind of revision of Christendom à la England under New World conditions and with reformed theological understanding.

Yet its kind of Christendom required a lot of doing. Settlers were not automatically Christians. Here was a Christendom which had to be realized through the Christianization of its inhabitants. This was due not only to the absence of a centuries-old settled society complete with parish system, but also to the peculiar nature of the Christianity being propagated by the leading clergy and lay people. A new requirement was being established, namely, that aspirants to membership give elaborate testimony to an experience of saving grace. This had a way of limiting church membership to those who meant business—and liked the way business was being conducted. Definitions and requirements such as these made for an ecclesiastical vigor, personal awareness, and sharp theological activity largely missing among the down-coast colonists. The Christian religion was genuinely planted in colonial New England; this differed from the South, where it bulked large as the option available if and when conditions were right. In New England it was an indispensable dimension of personal and social life.

New England's religious situation was, nevertheless, constantly changing. The logic of the church's own inner life was one cause of that; whenever you introduce the note of subjectivity as a decisive one in a theological system you reckon on self-assertion which leads to a dialogue resulting in modification of views, practices, and standards. A second contributing factor was the turning up, really from quite early years, of "dissidents" or "nonconformists," especially as the Middle Colonies became settled. Baptists, Anglicans, Jews, Roman Catholics, Quakers, and the Dutch Reformed were present by the middle of the seventeenth century or shortly thereafter. A little later Presbyterians arrived in sufficient quantity to demonstrate their intention to stay put; likewise Lutherans, Moravians, Anabaptists of one sort and another, and still more different groups landed between Delaware Bay and the Bay of Fundy. It should be noted, however, that these immigrations meant "change," not "fluidity," inasmuch as a normative tradition had deep roots, in the northeastern colonies particularly.

Secular forces too were making inroads into the holy commonwealth. By the middle of the eighteenth century, the process of transformation "from Puritan to Yankee" was tracking its inexorable course. Whereas, as Edmund Morgan has put it, theological categories and issues and religious leaders had provided the framework for living earlier, by 1790 or so political categories, issues, and leaders were doing so.[15] Not that politics displaced religion; instead, the providential world view was gradually exchanged for a more pragmatic and rational notion of the way things happen. Also as a by-product of this development, there commenced the related process by which religion became gradually more oriented toward the private areas of life. The traditional Christian's and the Calvinist's, hence the colonial Puritan's, vision of the truth entailed social, public responsibility for the church, as we have noted before. Stated directly, bringing God's sovereignty and will to bear on the public order was as much a suitable response as yielding one's heart to his grace and redemptive work. "Ethos and ethic" are basic categories for the entire American religious experience.

We are leaping well ahead of our story here; also a mis-impression may be registered, namely, that concern for public responsibility was disappearing when such was not the case. The point under discussion is that religion in the North just before and during Epoch A was "changing" and "mobile." It was moving from a previously solid form to a more diverse and precarious character. New England's religious outlook was being reoriented.

"Moving" is apt in more ways than one. Once the War for Independence was finished and the new American nation established, a sizeable proportion of New Englanders decided to leave the more settled (some said "stable") society of the seaboard for a venture into the West. Between 1790 and 1810 some of them trekked as far as 700 miles westward to begin life anew in western New York state and northern Ohio and Indiana. Their doing so signaled some important shifts in the culture; it also generated others. Once removed from the more delineated civilization these thousands found a need to adjust their religious forms. One expression was to neglect or forsake religion under the pressure of attending to daily necessities involved in building a new life in the face of formidable demands. Another was to transplant their old faith, with called-for modifications. Some became Methodists, or Methodist-like, as the enthusiasm of vital piety redirected their spiritual practices. Others remained Congregationalists or Presbyterians, but with church theology altered from its traditional Calvinism in the direction of free-will doctrine or "democratization." The scarcity of population and need to cooperate resulted in the Plan of Union of 1801, whereby "Presbygationalists" were produced. The two traditions had never been terribly far apart anyway; frontier conditions often brought forth an ecumenical spirit, especially in the early stages of frontier society where sectarianism was not an affordable luxury. In time, as the old frontier became itself the newest stage in the westward encroachment of the population, denomina-tionalism became important again, and cultural influences from the West came to make impact on life in the East.

It is helpful to know the anatomy of the Protestant faith these northern Christians inherited and then modified under new sociocultural conditions. For one thing, that way of interpreting the meaning of Christianity is important in its own right. But for our purposes here, it is critical to see how it diverged from its first-cousinly counterpart in the South. The distinction between the South's Evangelicalism and northern "Puritan Calvinism" (for want of a better label) may be hinted at as that between an individualist and a corporate theological orientation. But this leads to a second key difference, between epistemological positions where religious knowledge is compressed in the one case and diffused in the other.

Puritan Calvinism was just as emphatic as to the onto-logical distinction between the being of God and the being of his human creations as southern Evangelicalism. God is God and not creature; man is man and not Creator. An "in-finite qualitative difference" between God and each person characterized the understanding of both traditions. Simi-larly, both were forthright in acknowledging the finite, sin-ful, and fallen condition of man. Therefore, God's greatest concern was to rescue alienated humanity from the conse-quences of the fallen state in both this life and the one be-yond death. The atoning sacrifice of Christ on the cross was God's greatest gift in that it provided the means of escape for reconciliation with God. The theology of the Atone-ment was central to both systems of belief.

It is amazing how such congruency could have issued in so much divergence. A clue is contained in the ascription of centrality to one doctrine, Atonement. For what was more than central in the southern complex by being almost ex-clusively important, was merely central in the northern.

The northern set a far larger context, the three-dimensional completeness we have referred to earlier. Basic to the Puritan Calvinist view was the notion of fundamental corporateness to human life. While God created each individual (and each as an individual), he was believed to have created each as an individual in community with others. Salvation, accordingly, would be of all as well as of each, of the whole of life in society as well as of the human units which make it up. Furthermore, the very nature of the Christian life would be corporate (in the church), facilitated and sustained by others. Ongoing life in the body was as basic as entrance into it, more, indeed, than the moment of entry into it of which southern religion made so much. Implicit in the North's version was a conviction that one is always in the process of being made Christian; this lessened the emphasis on the conversion experience with its concomitant dramatic sense of assurance of pardon. And related in turn to that implication of process was the conviction that what Christians know they know in diffused fashion. They believed and committed themselves no less profoundly than the Evangelicals for whom religious knowledge was sure, direct, specific, precise—in a word, compressed. But their knowing was filtered through more mystery and spread out along a wider spectrum of convictions, awareness, and responsibilities, in a word, diffused. Whenever revivalism made its mark—of either the early frontier sort or in later "modern revivalism"—northern styles approximated the standard southern ones. Yet there was a difference even so, and one suspects it had to do with several factors, some of them seemingly extraneous, including the persistence of Puritan Calvinism's more comprehensive view of things and the North's continuing and growing heterogeneity, which meant that a revivalist mentality could never possess the religious mind of a region and be simply equated with Christianity.

A part of what has been said about developing new patterns refers to the western phase of the Second Awakening in the North. But the area of strength of that activity in the North in Epoch A was New England. Methodists were the earliest instigators, in the two decades on either side of 1800. McLoughlin summarizes their achievements: "The Methodists launched a vigorous campaign to win those disaffected from Hopkinsian Calvinism to their Arminian theology and their egalitarian form of church order. The circuit riding of Francis Asbury, Jesse Lee, and other zealous Methodist revivalists brought itineracy back into the settled parishes of New England and their camp meetings won many converts in the rural areas." Their main contribution, however, may have been to stir Congregationalism to new life, since for most New Englanders the "camp-meeting revivals of 1798–1808 were barbarous emotional outbreaks." [16]

The Congregational church, the extension of the old Standing Order in the emerging context of disestablishment, did have to put its mettle on the line. Its success was being challenged by these and other moderate enthusiasts from one angle and by Deism and Unitarianism from another. Of major importance for our purposes in this American cross-cultural study is how Congregationalism decided to go about withstanding the threats and even that it did so at all. Let us recall that religious organizations can fail and go out of business in the United States. Strategies for success based on assessments of needs and projected responsiveness became important when disestablishment became practically effective, and even earlier. In the South, the only concerted effort to do anything about the Church of England's failures up to this point had been undertaken about 1700, when its leaders in London realized that both white and black populations were being lost to them. The Methodist church in the late eighteenth century was sufficiently organized and mission-minded to take first steps toward organized crusades. But in the South it was not until the 1820s really that organized group planning became a staple among the denominations.

New England Congregationalism, though, assessd the situation of its society around 1800 and decided to act. It did so through its principal theologians. Timothy Dwight, president of Yale College, "appointed himself the champion of the old order." He and a few colleagues set out to save and reinforce the traditional church against the onslaught of alien forces. Their strategy quite naturally grew out of their perception of Christianity as a system of meaning which had a stable, Christian social order. In Robert Wiebe's words, "Easterners . . . still thought of churches as fixed institutions within an ordered society." [17] Accordingly, they appraised the state of affairs and worked to dissuade new-order people, especially the young, from following after false or misdirected ideologies. The least disruptive of these was that form promoted (more preached than taught) by the Protestant revivalists. Even this form, if allowed to seize the minds and hearts of the people, would wreak havoc with the "institutional order of decent society." Far more serious were the philosophies of Deism and Unitarianism, which, if left unchecked, would undermine the "very foundations of morality and stability." Itself a liberalized version of Protestantism, the new Unitarian church (1788) preached a less supernaturalistic message and attracted an impressive following in the better classes of society. Deism went much further, denying the authority of the Bible, the Incarnation, miracles, the efficacy of prayer, providential ordering of events, and human depravity requiring redemption. These deistic heresies, especially, had to be stopped.

The Reverend Mr. Dwight, a Congregationalist minister as well as educator and theologian, began to carve out a revised Calvinist interpretation of Christianity. That was the procedure deemed by him and a few colleagues as the proper route to head off religiously and socially pernicious currents abroad in the land. While the full fruits of this labor came two and three decades later with Lyman Beecher and Nathaniel W. Taylor as the chief gardeners, the agenda was set in Epoch A by Dwight and others who discerned that the old Calvinist theology was out of date and, consequently, worked to bring it into line with new sensibilities in the culture. Their most urgent assignment was somehow to soften the doctrine of the divine election and the limited Atonement views of "hyper-Calvinism" in favor of a more democratized, egalitarian, human free-will doctrine.

As far as South-North comparisons between 1795 and 1810 are concerned, a summary accounting lists some similarities and more dissimilarities, and, of weightier significance, few interactions and very little polarization. As a matter of fact, for this period there would be relatively little value in comparing the two areas (or otherwise analyzing them correlatively) but for the ineluctable fact that they belonged to a single nation. That they did meant that sooner and later, indirectly and directly, what each was and did religiously (and otherwise) affected the other, and most of all affected the whole, which in turn influenced each part. There is really no denying that inextricability and mutual influencing. But for the years 1795 to 1810, comparisons add up to little of salience. The united nation was not yet a unified culture. South and North experienced a minimum of actual cultural contact. Moreover, the South was only incipiently a militantly distinctive culture, hence no "North" as such existed. It is important to remember that there would not have been a "North" had there not been a South (the presence or absence of quotation marks is telling).

The South was shifting away from an establishmentarian condition in which the church, despite its enjoyment of a socially and legally favored position, was not very effective.

Before Independence the winds were blowing in the direction of evangelical Protestantism, although of a rather mild and certainly preinstitutionalized sort. The arrival of Epoch A meant that the die was cast in favor of Evangelicalism, now of a more radical and routinized variety, but still with a minimum of organization. The society we are talking about was still small and scattered in population, with most living on farms and the rest in quite small towns. Not only was this a preindustrial society, it was even preorganized, a kind of classic *Gemeinschaft* extended to the vast proportions of an entire region already 600 miles east to west and 700 miles north to south. In a setting like that, an expressive religious faith with freedom from organizationally and theologically fixed points is likeliest to be successful.

Paradoxically, as Mathews and T. Scott Miyakawa have taught us to see, it was this disorganized brand of religion which played so large a part in the building in of a sense of community and, in turn, of social arrangements and organizations. And what it unintentionally helped accomplish for the entire range of social institutions it also effected in church life, namely, centralized organization, although its ripening of this development came later. At this early stage, however, informal regularization was occurring; such forms as camp meetings and revivals were becoming the standard way of recruiting members—and recruitment was what there was at hand to do in an unsettled society on the far edges of Christendom. The southern states were a "fluid and flexible" situation at the beginning of Epoch A, but well on their way toward a crystallization of that condition into forms and styles which acquired a singular authenticity and became normative for the popular religion of the region.

The significance of the indigenous sects (denominations) which emerged during this period has not been adequately noted. It is important just that the O'Kelly and Stoneite movements (and to a lesser degree the Cumberland Presbyterian) came into being. But what is truly pungent is that these preached a message of no, or absolutely minimal, organization, certainly none that was centralized. In doing so, they drank more deeply (but only more deeply) than the others at the same republican well. Even they, however, could not completely escape a frontier version of Murphy's law, that whatever can become organized will become organized. From "fluid and flexible" to informally regularized and normative was the logic of the passage of southern religious culture.

The O'Kelly-Stone insistence that theology is not called for, only scriptural texts and proper congregational practice, is also of a piece with more general southern values. Methodists and Baptists did indeed have a theology, but it was readily transformed into a formula. Preachers had one message: Each is a sinner, Christ died for the sins of all, every person must repent and receive Christ in his or her heart for the forgiveness of sins and the gift of everlasting life. Some theological activity, that fraction of it done by city pastors mostly near the seaboard being the best, was to be undertaken later in the antebellum period. Also a spate of colleges was to appear from the 1820s down to the Civil War. The kind of frontier the South was, especially that beyond the Appalachians, however, did not nourish the reflective life. So, when problems arose in the society, there was no intellectual class to turn to for diagnosis and treatment. But then in a preformed society there were no societal problems, as such. The North—in particular, New England—was different.

In that society, conditions in religion were "changing and mobile." The western reaches of the North were only quantitatively different from the trans-Appalachian South; what distinguished the two was the anchor provided by the more settled New Englanders in the company of those relocating on the edge of a Christian civilization. The traditional notions of what constitutes proper church life and Christian responsibility to society underwent a process of alteration. The church was not spectacularly successful on the frontier. Where its vigor was manifested it tended to take Methodistic or de-Calvinized shape. But similar changes were also occurring back home in the anchor societies along the seaboard.

There was a society to be analyzed and there were people to do the analyzing. The best of the theological minds (who also entertained practical concerns) went to work on the problem. Their accustomed way was to present Christianity in better—that is, in more relevant, culturally sensitive—terms. This involved them in the founding stages of a new theology, the Arminianization of Calvinism. Human moral capacity to decide, act, and achieve was beginning to acquire a respect it had never known under Calvinist domination. And these early American "church planners" (social engineers?) had also to be apologists, for Deism as an alien theophilosophy and Unitarianism as a liberalized version of Protestantism were also potential claimants of the minds of the region.

As we have seen, something like "church planning" was going on in the South as well. But there it was a more instinctual, spontaneous technique for converting the lost, not something prescribed by a cadre of thinkers. Nevertheless, the two regions, despite numerous and very real differences, were caught up in the same process. It is deemed a "revitalization of culture" by McLoughlin, using Anthony Wallace's terminology. More specifically, developments in this period amounted to the declaration of cultural independence. Americans, southern and northern alike, were driven by their own new visions and by circumstances to wean themselves from European–eastern seaboard conventions to construct a national identity.

As far as regional differences are concerned, McLoughlin observes:

In the North, the Second Great Awakening challenged the older way of life at every turn, producing endless schisms and theological debates. In the South, after some initial denominational turmoil in the first decade of the century, this awakening confirmed the prevalent life style, increased religious homogeneity, and made the Methodists and Baptists so dominant that older sects were an almost invisible minority.

He terms the entire society "America's coming of age as a subculture; if it was not yet the equal, it was no longer the child of Europe."[18]

South and North, then, were "far" but "close" in the earliest years of the single society having two regional cultures. Interactions, interpenetrations, and direct reciprocal influences were few; their relation was a "far" one. But culturally they were "close," the people coming from the same stock, inheriting the same traditions, and indisseverably linked in the task of forming a new nation; and finally, joined in one federal union. The southern region was more a satellite to a magnetic moon than a central orbiting body. That angle of coordination was on its way toward monumental change, however. By Epoch B (1835–1850), it had become a pole unto itself, hoping unsuccessfully to manufacture its own orbit with satellites. In odd ways, as we are about to see, "far" became "near" and "close" remained "close" at the same time that polarization developed. And it all had to do with those Afro-American people, those slaves, who were not figuring very prominently in the cultural dynamics of the region as late as 1810.

TWO

Third Cousins Alienated
1835–1850

LOOKING BACK, WE MUST JUDGE THE QUARTER-CENTURY BE-
fore the War between the States to be the most enigmatic
period in the history of interregional relations. It is, of
course, also the most tragic. What made it enigmatic was
that South and North were so "near" and so "close" at the
very same time that animosity and antagonism were building so fractiously. Interaction ("near"-"far") between the
two regions was vigorous and, what is more significant, a
commonplace, right through 1860. *American* culture had
taken distinctive shape by this time; both regions participated in that and embodied it ("close"-"distant"). In a
great many respects they were nearly indistinguishable.
Simultaneously, war clouds were forming and before long,
the bloodiest battle ever fought by the American nation—
and the only one on its own soil—was being waged furious-
ly between those two parts of America, their "nearness" and
"farness" notwithstanding. A play on Vann Woodward's
depiction in *American Counterpoint* that "harmony is
based on dissonance as well as consonance" may be suggestive; only a national culture so united could be so
divided.[1]

How this uniting and dividing came about, what religion's role was in those occurrences, and what happened to
religious perspectives in the two regions through participation in that tumultuous period of American history is the

provenance of our inquiry into Epoch B. It goes without saying that that era is profoundly related, somehow, to Epoch A and the intervening quarter century. We have already glanced at how relatively weak southern identity was as late as 1810 (actually until 1820). Carl Degler notes that the appearance of a clear sense of regional identity came rather handily once the right circumstances were present to propel it, however. The seeds of divergence and discord were present from the colonial period in which already it was clear that life in the South differed from that in the North. They had lain dormant during "their years in national power," when also southern interests were not being threatened. Therefore we must be careful not to dramatize the awakening of southern identity about 1820, when the Panic of 1819 and the debate over the admission of Missouri to statehood precipitated the rousing of a regional sense which now for the first time was antagonistic. As Degler says, "The Missouri crisis was at once the identification of slavery as the basis of southern difference and a measure of the depth of southern identity." Well before our Epoch B, in other words, *South* was more than a geographical referent. It was an idea, a state of mind, an incipiently independent nation, a myth. In Degler's words again, "As early as the antebellum years North and South had created a *myth* of difference that went beyond the facts of difference."[2] "Near" and "close," "third cousins," yet alienated and, soon, belligerent. The paradox of "facts" and "myth" describes the real situation very well.

It all had to do with race. Given the long view and the reigning values of western civilization, one can only conclude that the South was the instigator, the agenda-setter, with "the North" existing only in response to there being a South. The point has been made a thousand times but no one has said it more tellingly than foreign visitors, in particular, Alexis de Tocqueville: "Were I inclined to continue this parallel, I could easily prove that almost all the differences which may be noticed between the characters of the Americans in the southern and northern states have originated in slavery."[3] Clement Eaton encapsulates the difference between the North and the South by the Jacksonian era as deriving from the "question of slavery"; this was the "greatest single cause for the emergence of the idea of a polarity of cultures existing between the two sections."[4]

In the South social arrangements, economic institutions, and philosophies all pivoting about racial matters penetrated life comprehensively. David Davis summarizes the point:

By the 1820s the institution of Negro slavery had come to dominate all aspects of Southern society. Apologies for slavery as an unfortunate though necessary evil were beginning to give way to aggressive self-justification. Paradoxically, as the South became increasingly isolated from the progressive ideology of the Western world, the rapid expansion of cotton cultivation helped to assure Southerners that their peculiar institution was indispensable to Northern and British industry. Accordingly, Southern slaveholders regarded their critics as ungrateful hypocrites who would literally bite the hand that fed them.[5]

Nor did the South see its advocacy of slavery as merely an economic gain for itself and others. Its program was morally consistent with the goals of the nation.

Although slavery had long been protected by various political and constitutional compromises, the compromises themselves rested on numerous tacit understandings. The North, for example, had accepted the legitimacy of slave property on the assumption that Southern leaders would do everything in their power to diminish and eventually eradicate the nation's moral burden. Beginning in 1820, sectional conflicts severely tested these understandings, and Southern leaders became increasingly convinced that their only security lay in fusing the expansion of slavery with America's republican mission. By portraying Britain as the chief enemy of slavery as well as of republican government, Southerners succeeded in wedding the cause of slavery with the nation's expanding "empire for liberty."[6]

The formulation of the ideological defense and advocacy of slavery was far advanced by 1835; in fact, it had crystallized, needing to harden only a little further before becoming the total system it had to become to eventuate in the secession of eleven states from the Union during the fall and winter of 1860–1861. Viewing conditions that way, however, tends to mislead us into thinking that southern identity was dominantly political, perhaps having relatively little to do with the popular culture. The truth of the matter is that the divergence of South from North began with economic and cultural factors rather than political. We should recall the South's participationist, even dominant, posture in national affairs through the Virginians' administrations, that is, through Jefferson's and Madison's (and to a degree Monroe's). Concerning the way things stood in 1819, Charles Sydnor remarks that while the South was "at peace with the nation on political issues, it was unlike it in many phases of its economic and social life." There were differences between the two regions, but only the most prophetic could have foreseen deep disturbances or open bitterness. He concludes: "Perhaps it is anachronistic to speak of Southerners at the beginning of the year 1819. The sense of oppression and the sectional patriotism that were soon to appear had not yet become visible."[7]

By 1835 they had. And there are few factors more transparent to the differences, actually to southern distinctiveness, than religion. To be sure, there is little evidence that religion served as a causative agent for what was occurring in southern society. Religion's conservative role in its fully extended proportions is an enduring quality of southern religious history, surely, as we shall be seeing piecemeal throughout and more elaborately in the final chapter. But while religion may have been causative of very little, it was a powerful force and one which tells us a great deal about the "mind of the South." There is a great deal of evidence that the southern story confirms Robert Bellah's axiom, "Every society is forced to appeal to some higher jurisdiction and to justify itself not entirely on its actual performance but through its commitment to unrealized goals or values."[8] Because the religious world view had gained such a firm hold on the southern imagination by the 1830s, it lay ready to hand as a source of meaning for interpreting and directing what was happening all around. Needless to say, the Bible itself was the locus classicus for that hermeneutical-moral exercise.

What was this southern society, this southern mind, and how did religion support it, legitimate it, and provide leverage for the interpretation of its place in history? How divergent was it from the nation at large, and in what ways? To begin with, we need to note how homogeneous southern society had become by Epoch B. This is seen, among other ways, in the depth and breadth of the South's commitment to slavery understood as economic system, as economic necessity, and as humane social arrangement. Notwithstanding slavery's being "an anomaly" in any part of the United States, "with its historic emphasis upon equality and freedom," and unlike the situation in other societies where slavery existed, it was defended as a reasonable part of the natural order of things.[9] Its status graduated from fact, to necessary evil, to necessity, to "this is our business," to positive good, and finally, to an issue worth fighting a war over. Furthermore, its acceptance—really, its being taken for granted—ran the gamut of the white population. Rather than being a commodity reserved for the better-off and resented by the have-nots, slavery was viewed as good for the society and slaveholding as a desirable condition by the great majority. Degler argues (against Eugene

Genovese, incidentally) that "the overwhelming majority of white Southerners accepted slavery and the values that surrounded it, because that kind of slavery served their interests as well as those of the slaveholders." His research reveals that the whites who did not own human property as a rule "aspired to become slaveholders themselves and to perpetuate the world slavery had made."[10] Slaves, slavery, and slaveholding were part and parcel of southern society. It is true that there were exceptions to this rule, people and philosophies emerging from the southern context who called the whole business into question on constitutional, theological, or humanitarian grounds. Cassius M. Clay of Kentucky and Hinton R. Helper of North Carolina are prime examples, the former for more idealistic reasons, the latter having in mind more pragmatic, economic concerns. By and large, though, slavery was as much an aspect of southern society as Thomas Jefferson, the city of Charleston, a rural way of life, and evangelical Christianity.

The social homogeneity is seen also in the religious life of the people. Clement Eaton highlights this condition in his observations that "by 1830 the southern people had become thoroughly converted to orthodoxy in religion,"[11] and on the eve of the Civil War they were "on the whole a deeply religious people."[12] The statistical picture is provided for us by Sydnor:

Between 1820 and 1850 the membership of the Methodist Church in Virginia, the Carolinas, and Georgia increased from 93,000 to 223,713 and of the Baptist Church from 99,000 to 246,000, while the aggregate population of these four states increased only one-third. The Episcopalians and Presbyterians were also growing, though not in such numbers; and west of the mountains the churches were making great gains.[13]

There were, of course, other denominations present in the South. The colonial plantings of Catholics, Lutherans, Moravians, Mennonites and Brethren, Congregationalists,

Quakers, and others had survived, not to mention the relatively flourishing "Christian" and Cumberland Presbyterian sects. Most of these, however, served specific ethnic or historically special communities (over many decades a fair proportion of individuals within these married into or "converted" to the popular regional churches).

In general, the South had come under the rule of an evangelical hegemony. Virtually everybody believed in the Bible and that Christianity's message was all about personal salvation from sin for heaven. One measure of the relative uniformity of belief, paradoxically, is the Presbyterian departure from it. The southern Calvinists were not one whit less convinced of the absolute inerrancy and exclusive authority of Scripture than their more populous fellow Protestant bodies. They also defined meaning in the terms of depravity, Atonement, forgiveness, and pardon. The primary divergence came at the point of the *experience* of conversion, the Presbyterians placing far more stock in baptism, the objective conferral of grace, and a process of regeneration than in an emotional experience of conversion. Yet the basic thrust of Christian meaning and responsibility was fairly constant. In addition, we must underscore that these beliefs were as likely to be held by the unchurched as by the churched. This was a regional society's perspective on the truth. A consensus prevailed.

Our nation's most perceptive foreign visitor-analyst, de Tocqueville, found this religious condition to be more than a consensus, however. It was another instance of the "tyranny of the majority," one which enlarged greatly during Epoch B. Eaton tells us that:

In 1831–32 de Tocqueville had found little essential difference between the North and the South in respect to tolerance. He observed that whether he traveled in the northern or the southern states, the voice of the majority exercised a remarkable dictatorship over the minds of American citizens, especially oppressing those who held unorthodox religious opinions. Such a tyranny of public opinion, operating completely outside of the realm of law, he noted, contrasted with the free political institutions of the Americans. By the 1850s the northern states seem to have attained a freer intellectual climate with regard to religion and social reforms; the South, in the meanwhile, had regressed in the matter of intellectual freedom.[14]

The interweaving of the society's attitude toward slavery and the popular religious perceptions made for a strong social fabric. By now religion was entrenched; it took a definitive shape during this period. Slavery was the basis of the economic, hence the social and political, life of the society. The tensile strength of each was formidable; the interweaving made for virtual unbreakability. Two instances of their correlation must suffice here to indicate how much force they wielded. One is the slave codes, governing Negroes' opportunities in education and religion, the other is the Mission to the Slaves organized by the Methodist church and copied in a variety of ways by other Christians intent on taking the Christian message to the Afro-American heathen.

Slave codes were passed by all the southern states to regulate the behavior of the enslaved people. That these codes should extend over all civil rights made sense under the system, but the limits were being stretched when they were applied to civic privileges like education and worship. These two ventures of the human spirit were bound to be linked, after all, in a society that accorded a certain ancient collection of writings so much credence. Stanley Elkins outlines this aspect of the supervision of blacks' behavior:

Every southern state except Maryland and Kentucky had stringent laws forbidding anyone to teach slaves reading and writing, and in some states the penalties applied to the educating of free Negroes and mulattoes as well. It was thought that "teaching slaves to read and write tends to dissatisfaction in their minds and to produce insurrection and rebellion"; in North Carolina it was a crime to distribute among them any pamphlet or book, not excluding the Bible. The same apprehensions applied to instruction in religion. Southern society was not disposed to withhold the consolations of divine worship from its slaves, but the conditions would have to be laid down not by the church as an institution, not even by the planters as laity, but by planters simply as masters.[15]

The more extreme of these proscriptive actions came in the wake of insurrections small and large occurring in the 1820s and culminating in Nat Turner's slave revolt of 1831. (Both insurrections and regulations dated as far back as the 1790s.) Slaveholders and virtually all other whites as well were terrified at the double prospects of the threatened destruction of the economic system and the loss of order and tranquility, perhaps even of life. Religion was seen as both cause and cure of this horrendous situation—cause when the religion was misguided, as in the case of the possessed preacher Turner, and cure when it was Christianity "properly" taught to the slaves in organized religious instruction.

A dynamic and sometimes volatile social condition and a worried, even tortured, white conscience is revealed through some slaveholders' attitudes as reported by Elkins. J. W. Fowler of Mississippi welcomed the preaching of the gospel to his slaves provided that they could hear it "in its original purity and simplicity." He instructed his overseer to be present any time preaching took place, in church or elsewhere, "in view of the fanaticism of the age." A Savannah slaveowner, Alexander Telfair, issued similar instructions to his overseer; there was to be "no night-meeting or preaching . . . allowed on the place except on Saturday night and Sunday morn." State laws frequently made it unnecessary, formally at least, for owners to take such matters into their own hands. South Carolina forbade religious meetings of slaves or free Negroes "either before the rising of the sun or after the setting of the same." Mississippi law permitted attendance at preaching only if the preaching were by a white minister and if authorization to attend had been granted by one's master.[16]

Such laws, which served to compound the intricacies of an already complex system, reflected desperation in a white population which nevertheless felt impelled to present Christianity to the Afro-American heathen in their midst. It did offer that presentation to a great host of them, successfully in thousands of cases, as the increase in the number of black Methodists and Baptists in the decades before emancipation indicates. For the Methodists the figures (probably inflated) are 118,904 in 1846 and 209,836 in 1861; for the Baptists, a doubling of the 1845 figure over the next fifteen years. Pleas were issued, funds were raised, and energies were expended toward the goal of saving the souls of those whom God in his Providence had wrested from a pagan land and given the whites for their caring. Quite naturally, then, the churches frequently deplored the legal restrictions clamped on this holy responsibility. But, as Elkins summarizes it, "The church could do nothing. Its rural congregations were full of humane and decent Christians, but as an institution of authority and power it had no real existence."[17] Mathews shows us, however, how convoluted the situation was in his observation that "the Christian churches were the only institutions in the South which could and did speak for the Negro."[18]

The multiplicity of motives leading to white missionary activities among black people is consistent with the larger picture being painted here; that is to say, it shows how torn —tortured may be more accurate—the southern white mind was over the anomalous condition it was working diligently to sustain. Raboteau addresses the question of motivation in this passage:

In all the reports, resolutions, minutes, sermons, and speeches devoted to the plantation-mission cause, several kinds of motives were expressed by planters and missionaries. The desire to evangelize the poor, the desire to make slaves docile, the desire to create a model plantation, and the desire to defend slavery against abolitionist attacks were all reasons for supporting plantation missions. In addition . . . there was another reason moving laymen and clergy alike, although this reason remained largely unexpressed. Not only was Christianization of the slaves a rationale for slavery, but it was, as it had been from the beginning, a balm for the occasional eruptions of Christian conscience disturbed by the notion that maybe slavery was wrong.[19]

No matter whether the incentive was conscience, or evangelistic zeal, or social need for law and order, or something else, the task of Christianizing the slaves was undertaken with notable intensity.

The best-known and organized enterprise established for the purpose of bringing slaves to Christianity was the Methodists' Mission to the Slaves begun in the 1830s and operated down to the schism of 1844 which resulted in the formation of the Methodist Episcopal Church, South. Associated most prominently with the name of the Reverend William Capers (later bishop) and concentrated in coastal South Carolina and Georgia, this was an official agency of the Methodist church. Mathews calls it "the institutional symbol of the Methodists' special concern" and "the Church's conscientious alternative to anti-slavery activity."[20] It was a part of the church's missionary outreach activities which also included an overseas division and another for sending missionaries to the Indians throughout the United States. With reference to work with Negroes, the first formal efforts were undertaken through the South

Carolina Conference. Gradually the field of such work enlarged and became more organized, culminating with Capers's appointment in 1840 as secretary of the new Southern
Department of Missionary Work of the Methodist Episcopal Church. Its peak year was 1844, the last, because that
was the final year of a united American Methodism. Capers
and Bishop James O. Andrew of Georgia, the focal figure
in the schism, owing to his refusal to free his slaves and
northern Methodists' unwillingness to tolerate a slaveholding bishop, had led in establishing the Mission throughout
the South. They had been joined by "missionaries, planters, and Methodist journals in New York, Richmond, Nashville, Charleston, and Cincinnati. . . . Eighty Methodist
missionaries working in every southern state cared for over
22,000 slave members and preached to thousands more."[21]
The entire undertaking was a difficult one, straining
church-slave owner relations, making large demands of the
missionaries, and running into numerous financial problems. But, withal, as the "institutional symbol of the Methodists' special concern," it was a rather effective undertaking.

Raboteau outlines the typical approach taken by the
Methodists and other denominations in providing religious
instruction for the slaves through what he terms "a practical
method . . . deemed prudent and appropriate for southern
circumstances."

The first step was regular preaching to the slaves on the Sabbath with sermons geared to "their level of understanding."
Secondly, a lecture was to be held once a week during the eve-
ning, or . . . one or two plantation meetings could be held for
slaves in connection with regular pastoral visitations of white
church members. . . . Thirdly, Sabbath schools should be organized for children, youths, and adults. Fourthly, instruction
was to be by the oral method (using catechisms, homilies, and
audio-visual aids). . . . Fifthly, "stated seasons for gathering together all colored members" of the church were strongly rec-
ommended. . . . Finally, no plantation meeting should ever be

held without the knowledge and express consent of the owner
or manager of the place.[22]

Like every other aspect of white Christians' dealings with
Negroes, this story is one of mixed motives, torn loyalties,
defensive actions, and tortured reasoning. Charles Grier Sellers has written cogently on this "travail of slavery," a tragic
condition highlighted by the question of whether the slave
was a person or merely property.[23] Many whites did desire
the transformation of the Afro-Americans from pagan religions to the true faith, but on terms to be dictated by white
society. Yet some noble efforts were made and some impressive accomplishments resulted. One form of the latter was
the composition of the catechisms earlier referred to, most
notably Capers's *Short Catechism for the Use of the Colored
Members on Trial of the Methodist Episcopal Church in
South Carolina,* and *A Catechism for Colored Persons* by
Charles Colcock Jones. The member of a distinguished,
wealthy Georgia family, Jones was a Presbyterian minister
trained at Princeton and South Carolina College, who
worked tirelessly and creatively to bring Christianity to the
slaves and to build a biracial community. The examples and
printed materials provided by these two men were influential throughout the South for nearly three decades. Through
them, the organized efforts mentioned, and numerous other
activities, Negro slaves, free Negroes, and mulattoes were
made acquainted with the Christian religion by those who
owned or dominated them and sought to convert and instruct them from a variety of motives. Summarizing and
forecasting, we may say that the whole southern population
came to live within Christianity's framework, with results
as complex and unintended as the motives were mixed.

Earlier allusions to "nearness" and "closeness" between
these "third cousins" on their way to alienation call for
more extensive treatment. Actually, however, our discussion
of the interweaving of firm and well-nigh ubiquitous racial

attitudes and religious practices has been edging us toward that treatment. Perhaps at first glance this development in southern culture appears to distance the South and the North from each other so that both interaction and cultural overlap are prevented. That pattern of regional correlation was to surface after the Civil War (our Epoch C—"strangers in same household") as never before or since, but not in the anomalous and tragic years of Epoch B. Curiously, the very issue of the church and slavery was rendered an institutional dilemma by regional interaction. In the Methodist case, northern and southern members belonged to the same church in a connectional system; Baptists in the two regions held membership in the same Convention where the unity was based on and epitomized by cooperative missionary endeavors. Moreover, it was the very fact of their joint heritage in one culture which made their divergence on questions of value so traumatic. They were still cousins, after all. Family metaphors aptly describe the relations, down to the era when immigration created a nation which could build unity around its constitution but no longer through common, widely shared ethnic traditions. Tragically, the South was the section of the country where the family metaphor first failed to accord with the real societal conditions; blacks and whites were hardly cousins (except in those not too infrequent instances of miscegenation). Putting the problems of southern society that way helps illuminate the anguished character of existence there. A "homogeneous" society was forced to find structural—impersonal, antifamilial—modes for carrying on its life. It did so, but not very naturally and far from gracefully.

Yet in order to see the fuller picture, we must observe that South and North were experiencing a great deal of "nearness." John Hope Franklin's book, *A Southern Odyssey,* veritably rings the changes on the extent and significance of interaction between the people of the two cultures to a point within a few weeks of the secession movement in late 1860. Some of it was northerly in direction, Southerners going to the North, and much of it was reciprocal, but there were few surges purely southerly in direction. A major example of South looking North was in the recreational travel of well-off Southerners to northern cities, centers of high culture, baths and spas, and scenic attractions. Sometimes they combined business with pleasure, but most often they journeyed to enjoy the more culturally advanced centers and to take advantage of the more diverse and colorful facilities available in the North. A variety of modes of transportation was available, but going by train was especially common, and the railroad lines encouraged this choice with invitingly low fares.

Going north for post-secondary education was a surprisingly common practice for young men from the better classes of southern society. Southern enrollees were disproportionately represented in the student bodies of Princeton and West Point, but conspicuous in a number of other places as well: Harvard, Yale, and the law schools of those two institutions plus Litchfield and Columbia. Other colleges too attracted a small number of men from the South, as did several of the North's military schools, and a few young ladies attended northern academies. Medical education being sparsely available in the South, most of the region's physicians were trained in the major northern institutions. The story of southern people from the privileged, leading classes who chose to expose themselves to the North's alternate style of living is quite a long one.

Reciprocity, of a sort, characterized the economic interaction of the two regions. Whenever progressive Southerners were promoting industrial development in the region, they did so with northern accomplishments as model and inspiration. Obviously a number had been North and seen for themselves the advantages (and liabilities also) of indus-

tries there. Their region lagged behind in economic development. Yet the South was providing goods, cotton and tobacco being high on a moderately long list. This did not
offset the disadvantage at which the South stood in the relation, however. The means and routes of transportation by
which southern people and goods ventured to New York,
Philadelphia, Niagara Falls, and Boston existed because of
northern capital and initiative. Southern merchants by the
hundreds journeyed to the national centers of manufacture
and distribution, almost all of them outside their own region. Additionally, the better classes of society learned that
the best clothes, home furnishings, some farm necessities,
and much more could be selected from larger inventories,
for lower prices, and with better credit than at home or near
by. Finally, the printing and publishing industry was the
North's in a virtual monopoly. Many other commodities
and services were at least available in the South, but on this
front there was no competition.[24]

In his 1968 Lamar Lectures, *The Role of the Yankee in
the Old South,* Fletcher Green showed that many Yankees
came South, perhaps a half-million moving that way between 1776 and 1860. A notable proportion of leaders in
southern churches and church-related colleges were transplanted Yankees. Transylvania, Hampden-Sydney, and Bay-
lor are among the colleges which were so benefited. The list
of clergymen who were originally Northerners is most impressive: Marshall, Furman, Quintard, Meredith, Sher-
wood, McGready, Bascom, Gildersleeve, and many others
in all the major denominations. Yet this phenomenon argues some constructive points and negates others. How
many came and how easily they came to be at home in the
South confirms the social unity of the nation, that ambigu-
ous fact we are observing in a number of aspects. At the
same time, Green's research reveals that those who came
and stayed were those who were assimilated; the price of

assimilation was the loss of "alien" identity, achieved largely through complicity in the South's acceptance of slavery.[25]

Illustrations of South-North interaction proliferate beyond these brief recitations. The extent, and especially the peculiar character of the religious interactions are of greatest interest to us here. We have already observed that the fact of Methodist and Baptist relatedness, indeed of organizational alliance, is what occasioned grief, then bitterness, and ultimately division in those two denominations. A few details of that story are now called for.

The General Conference of the Methodist Episcopal Church, meeting in New York City in May 1844, brought things to a head. Southern Methodists withdrew from the united national body and over the next several months worked to organize themselves into a regional church, their efforts coming to fruition in May 1845. The general issue which set the context for national thinking that year was the admission of Texas; was it to be a slave state or a free state? What precipitated the schism in Methodism was a much smaller but highly symbolic issue, the fact that the Bishop of Georgia, James O. Andrew, owned slaves. The peculiar circumstances of his slaveholding, namely, that he had been bequeathed two Negro children who could not be manumitted under Georgia law, and that his second wife owned slaves, did not mollify northern Methodists. Nor were the tensions relieved by his going to the trouble of making the legal arrangement of securing them to her by a deed of trust. Andrew's next decision was that he should resign, but a meeting of the southern caucus noted that he could not do that. Following a lengthy and heated series of debates, the Conference took formal action, approved by the delegates from both regions, to separate the church into two parts. The Methodist connectional system necessitated the schism of South from North.[26]

The Baptist separation was less complex and disruptive

because the previous linkage was less fundamental. Mathews summarizes this event thus:

> After 1840, Southern Baptists were becoming increasingly restive because of abolitionism of many of their northern coreligionists. Southerners complained that northern Baptists did not accept them on the basis of "entire social equality." Therefore, in November, 1844, the Alabama Baptist state convention demanded that the Board of Managers of the Baptist General Convention explicitly avow that slaveholders were as eligible to become missionaries as were nonslaveholders. . . . The Baptist officials . . . explained unequivocally that they could "never be a party to any arrangement which would imply approbation of slavery." Because Northerners would not affirm Negro servitude as an amoral act of life acceptable to all Baptists, dissidents formed the Southern Baptist Convention in 1845.[27]

These occurrences did far more than separate a million and a half Methodists and a similar number of Baptists from their northern brethren. They added to increased sectional antagonism, contributing one more weight to the load that in the 1860s would break the bridge and create a second nation for a short time and an alienated southern regional society and culture for many decades. The previously united Methodist denomination was not to realize that "nearness" again until 1939. The once affiliated Baptists have remained "far" now for more than a century.

No minor cause of the two religious schisms was the growing abolitionist fervor in the North and the "national fervor for reform."[28] In cases like these the "nearness" had an ironic aspect in part and was partly the result of reaction. One wonders what the course of nineteenth-century history would have been had not "extremists," the aggressive advocates of ending slavery in American society, pushed their program. Quite apart from any wide-ranging speculation, we may be pretty certain that the denominational schisms would have come about later and less acrimoniously. A major instance of irony in the "nearness" of South and

North is pointed up in Raboteau's comment that "abolitionist arguments against slavery challenged proslavery
apologists to push slave evangelization as one of the strongest proofs that slavery was a positive good."[29] The logic of
these developments was sealed by the fact that once the
southern Methodists and Baptists had declared their auton-
omy, they were obligated "to live up to the ideals for which
they had seceded."[30] Having insisted that the condition of
slavery was conducive to the Christianization of Negroes,
they had to redouble their efforts to bring that about.

A similar point was made by the reaction of some southern Christian leaders to the various reform movements taking place in the nation, South and North, much of it tied in
with church activities. As the concern over the mission to
the slaves was building toward crescendo, Charles Colcock
Jones perceived that movement as possessing the aura of a
"social gospel." He insisted that the "urgent need of the
slaves at home to have the Gospel preached to them" was
akin to the enterprises symbolized by the existence of the
United Evangelical Front. He viewed working with the
slaves as one of many "interdenominational efforts to make
America holy by means of home and foreign mission societies, Bible and tract societies, and temperance and Sabbath School societies."[31] Clearly, he was aware of what was
happening beyond as well as within the region and, for
whatever set of reasons, sought to classify this reform-mind-
ed activity as part of something that was happening in the
nation at large.

While it is impossible to discern Jones's incentives in
making that classification, one is inclined more to the view
that he was aware of national moral currents than that he
saw the same things happening South as North. In this respect the two regions were "nearer" than they were "close"
at this time. In point of fact, the South had played an impressive role in social reform movements earlier on, espe-

cially in the first two decades of the nineteenth century. Together with the northern United States, it had participated in a variety of reform movements, such as the "abolition of imprisonment for debt, temperance, and the expansion of suffrage."[32] Public higher education was more widespread and better supported South than North. "Even the number of antislavery societies in the South as late as 1820 exceeded that in the northern states." Degler is brought to the conclusion that "save for the southern defense of slavery, it is difficult to find political or social values that were dominant in the North that were not also widely present and deeply held in the South."[33] But that was early in the century. The compulsion to defend slavery changed all that. Degler correlates the earlier and later situation:

> The antebellum years constituted a veritable ferment of reform in the United States, in which, during the first two decades of the nineteenth century, the South participated. But under the impact of the need to defend slavery against an increasingly hostile northern and world opinion, Southerners found advocacy of reform potentially threatening. To open up to challenge any facet of the social order might well cause slavery itself to be brought into question or placed under attack. Nor was the reasoning wholly paranoid. If a southern eye were cast northward it was plain that many reformers who were active in behalf of women's rights, the peace movement, or new community organizations, were generally also antislavery in their outlook.[34]

Sydnor renders the concern of Southerners with building a more perfect society even more impressive by focusing on the southern, not merely American or European, roots of such reform efforts. "During the Revolutionary period men had set out to establish a more perfect democracy, end slavery, ameliorate prison conditions, establish schools and colleges, enlarge economic opportunities, and provide complete religious freedom." While the running, developing, and improvement of social amenities and facilities con-

tinued in the Old South, the reform movement, characterized by that spirit and vigorous, "lost momentum before all
its goals were reached." By the years of Epoch B, Southerners had moved to Jones's position of affirming southern
perfection and of claiming that their own age was the gold-
en age.[35] Charles Colcock Jones, I repeat, was probably
more aware than assertive, with the absence of a social program rendering his hopefulness somewhat naive, than an
accurate reporter of what reform really was or was not in
his society.

In the contemporaneous North, the thirty years before
the war was the era of vigorous reform. The social evils and
problems we have already noted as marking the southern
scene were being addressed. As we shall see, many more
which arose from societal conditions peculiar to the North
were being attacked as well. Slavery was only one of these
many. For the most part it existed as a problem only because it was a problem in the South, hence for the nation.
To describe the North's enjoining the matter of slavery in
this way is not meant to diminish its importance, but rather
to call attention to the fact that it was more a moral issue
than an immediately practical problem. For the North,
slavery was a concern by reaction. By 1830 the number of
slaves in the North had been reduced to some 3600, most
of them in New Jersey and Delaware. The Negro population in all the northern states stood at 167,000. Northern
society was not preoccupied with slavery, largely because
there were so few slaves living in its midst. Yet there was
the problem, and, what was increasingly important, there
was the South. In Woodward's words, "As the sectional
crisis intensified in the 1850s . . . the South, not the Negro,
came to be regarded as the real menace to the North."[36]
For northern society the problem surfaced more as the existence of a nation with two antagonistic regions than as
troublesome conditions under its own nose. As pieces of the

westward-stretching territory manifestly destined to belong to the United States had to be considered for admission to statehood, an issue became a problem. As never before, North and South were made aware of their unity in a single nation.

As for the northern churches' involvement with slavery, it would be too much to say that revivalism was generally being transformed into one large antislavery crusade. For one thing, evangelistic efforts were continuing in many of the region's cities and through ongoing camp meetings. Moreover, organized activities to convert people to antislavery could never be quite the same as programs for converting lost sinners to faith in Christ. Nevertheless, in what was a dramatic new venture, the Reverend Theodore Weld and a circle of ministers and theological students around him carried the antislavery message with zeal and Christian justification to many places in the near Midwest, using revivalism's format as their approach. They, along with Charles G. Finney, Lyman Beecher, Lane Theological Seminary, and Oberlin College helped spearhead an effective (and sometimes vituperative) campaign against slavery in the North. Organized abolitionist movements often made their attacks on slavery in purely religious terms; it was evil, contrary to the will of God, hence it must be purged from the land and its perpetrators converted from their wicked practice of slaveholding.

Yet reactions to slavery among the people of the North were varied. Doubtless most, going about the business of living their lives in private spheres, paid little heed to this issue which was sorely testing the unity of the nation. But a number were actually racists who advocated slavery. One incentive was the fear of a North inundated by fugitive or liberated Negroes. An invasion of blacks might very well "fill the jails and poorhouses, compete with white labor, and degrade society."[37] As a consequence of such fears, numerous antiabolition mobs stalked the North in the 1830s and 1840s. Leonard Richards's research discloses the makeup of these northern agitations against organized efforts to eradicate slavery. "They were neither revolutionary nor lower-class. They involved a well-organized nucleus of respectable, middle-class citizens who wished to preserve the status quo rather than to change it. . . . Sometimes they represented the Establishment. More frequently they *were* the Establishment."[38]

Social restiveness, then, was an undiscriminating visitor to both northern and southern societies in our Epoch B. The South's slavery—which, let us not forget, as a property right was guaranteed by the Constitution—was a common denominator in this continuity. South and North were "near" in that developments and conditions in one caused perturbations in the other. And they were "close" in more fundamental ways than common knowledge has supposed. They shared many of the same values, including approbation of slavery sometimes, because, after all, they were still ethnically kin and politically one. David Potter makes the case, though perhaps a bit excessively, in this passage on the state of the two regional societies during the 1850s:

There was still a vigorous Union nationalism remaining in the South, and in spite of all the emotional fury, there was probably more cultural homogeneity in American society on the eve of secession than there had been when the Union was formed, or than there would be a century later. Most Northerners and most Southerners were farmer folk who cultivated their own land and cherished a fierce devotion to the principles of personal independence and social equalitarianism. They shared a great pride in their Revolutionary heritage, the Constitution and "republican institutions," and an ignorance about Europe, which they regarded as decadent and infinitely inferior to the United States. They also shared a somewhat intolerant, orthodox Protestantism, a faith in rural virtues, and a commitment to the gospel of hard work, acquisition, and success.[39]

Given both the "nearness" and the "closeness" of the two regions during Epoch B and right up to the war, the trage- dy of the internecine strife of the one nation bulks dramat- ically large. It may even seem, in retrospect, to have been totally uncalled for. Yet there were basic, festering, and en- larging differences, political, economical, cultural, and, not least, religious. To what degree religious factors (or any others) "caused" the differences it is impossible, and un- necessary, to decide. But they were there and they played a part. The splintering of the largest denominations is indi- cation of that. It helps to see the emergence of the Method- ist Episcopal Church, South, and the Southern Baptist Convention as instances of cultural-religious indigenous- ness. While both were part of much more extensive and long-formed interpretations of Protestant Christianity, they were also fruits of southern culture in a very real sense. The Baptists especially reflected southern modes and sensibili- ties (and do profoundly to this day), owing mostly to the looseness of the ties which had linked them with their northern brethren. The Methodists of the South at that time, in the intervening years, and today show fewer dis- tinguishing marks of regional culture, but regional differ- ences are apparent.

Carrying the theme of indigenousness one step farther, we note also the contrast between these southern sources and indigenous forms of Christianity and their northern counterparts. Those forms were already the central ones in southern church life, hence they sprang from the very heart and soul of regional culture. In the North, a spate of in- digenous forms appeared or grew toward maturity during Epoch B, most notably the Mormons and Adventists. "Out west" in upstate New York, revival fires swept widely enough to create a veritable "burned over district." Having soured on the traditional forms of Christianity transplanted here from Europe, and imbued with the apocalyptic spirit of a new stage in history symbolized by the emergence of the American nation, they determined to start from scratch. Adventism was closer to traditional Christianity by quite a lot than the Church of Jesus Christ of Latter-Day Saints, but both claimed a grand, fresh vision. Mormonism, which we may justly term a religious epitomization of America, moved with its indigenous perceptions and values to a radically divergent theology. In its own more moderate (if also eccentric) fashion, Adventism struck out on a course rather far removed from that of the reigning interpretations— Presbyterian, Congregationalist, Methodist, and the like. The South's homespun separate organizations were as predictable, identifiable, and "down home" as one can imagine. The North's were bold and innovative, even weird and pernicious.

Closer to the center of American cultural and religious life throughout the first half of the nineteenth century was Evangelicalism (in its broad denominational array) with its focus on the conversion experience. The need to bring sinners to repentance and conversion in an essentially frontier society was no respecter of regions. In North and South alike, camp meetings and revivals were attuned to bringing a potentially faithless society into the Christian fold. Not that there were not differences, however. These were quantitative, emanating from divergent emphases, two in particular. The South disdained social activism because of its theology, which was linked to a hands-off policy concerning slavery, while northern revivalism saw social reform as Christian business, sometimes through direct political action, sometimes not. The second difference stems from northern revivalism's more optimistic anthropology. Sanctification and perfectionism were preached and especially widely accepted after 1830, about the same time that the South's orthodoxy of sin and guilt acquired an unbreakable hold. Each viewpoint was correlated with prevalent social conditions. In the North, all signs pointed toward endless progress; toward building the Kingdom of God on earth. The South had a fixation on its individualism, on the need for supernatural deliverance, and on the ravages of sin in human life.

These distinctions are well illustrated by attitudes toward entry into the Christian life. Recent research by Jon Alexander has disclosed a significant divergence after 1825 in southern and northern patterns of conversion, following a period of remarkable, seemingly stylized similarity.[40] In Alexander's own words, the accounts of such experiences are "strikingly similar" across regional boundaries down to 1825. The process of conversion generally followed this route:

(1) a life-threatening experience which led to (2) serious thought about religion; (3) efforts at self-reformation; (4) doubts about the self; (5) despair; (6) docility; (7) conversion; (8) testing, confirmation and commitment. Converts both North and South heard voices and Scripture, dreamed of hell, felt the presence of demonic and angelic powers, contemplated suicide, attended revivals, sobbed in public and private prayer, were chided and encouraged by associates, and were encouraged by the conversion of others.

The examination of numerous autobiographical and narrative accounts reveal that similarity gave way to regular differences with the coming of the century's second quarter. First, in the South, conversion became "more uniform and controlled. Voices, visions, dreams, and physical struggles with the devil were less frequently reported by White converts." In Weberian terms, a process of "routinization" was setting in. This development was coordinated with the virtual monopoly Evangelicalism was gaining in the South. We are not surprised to learn then that "published conversion accounts which depart from the Evangelical pattern are rare."

Second, a kind of routinization set in in the North as well. Alexander summarizes it this way: "The harsh despair and the radical change of life described in earlier accounts was giving way to an experience of sweetness and support more gradual in its operation." And what is of greatest importance is the fact that "the earlier struggle with the self was increasingly replaced by a commitment to struggle for social reform." We may indeed see this as routinization, but the new feature in the picture is that what was being routinized was no longer the dominant pattern of religious life in northern society. Evangelicalism was becoming less evangelical; that is, other interpretations of Christian meaning were claiming a foothold among northern Protestants, at the same time that Protestantism as a whole was "sharing its place with other religious expressions." Among these were Mormonism (so radical as to require its own special classification), Unitarianism, and Transcendentalism at the liberal and very liberal stations on the spectrum, and Roman Catholicism (about which more presently), the epitome of traditionalism. A clue to the greater infrequency of and loss of dominance by Evangelicalism is provided by the observation that a greater number of spiritual autobiographies was published by Northerners than by Southerners in this period. Alexander notes that there would seem to be a kind of general law that "spiritual autobiographies are written by persons whose religious experience is seen by the culture in which it takes place as unusual." Thus, significant changes are occurring in the northern scene simultaneously with the South's entrenchment. Religion, and a particular, stylized form of religion at that, has taken over the field in the homogeneous South; in the North Evangelicalism was only one form of religious life and even its position was being altered.

Alexander speaks of the northern evangelical conversion experience as "becoming more gradualistic and developing

an increasing social dimension." He reaches the following
overall conclusion:

Before the 1850s the Evangelical conversion experience in both
the South and the North was fundamentally similar. After 1825
the Evangelical conversion experience achieved dominant position in the Southern religious scene while in the North the
Evangelical conversion became one of many religious currents.
Where Evangelical conversion in the North tended to propel
converts into social reform in the South it tended to bring converts a feeling of contentment.

The relative similarity of southern and northern religious
practice down to the 1850s must be emphasized. The era of
Epoch B and a few years before and after have been rightly
called "the Methodist Age" by students of American church
history focusing primarily on the North. Evangelicalism
was indeed the growing edge of Christianity in the North
in those years. After that there was true divergence—as our
examination of Epoch C will disclose. Differences appeared
after 1825, but not yet a basic divergence. "Closeness" still
prevailed; the power of centrifugal forces had only begun
to demonstrate strength. In this way, regional religious life
affords insight into the development of "two radically different cultures in a fundamentally similar society."

   Yet another irony has been lurking below the surface of
this last explicit analysis. The South was becoming a society, homogeneous in its patterns of culture and united in
its progression toward separate political identity. During
that development, however, its dominating religious forms
"went private." Religion was seen as primarily a matter of
the individual's standing before God, who would grant or
withhold the pardon of sins and the reward of everlasting
life, and of the sinner's relationship with the Lord, emanating in assurance and consolation. The theme of responsibility for the public order, or for prophetic scrutiny into
society's ways, was rarely struck by the churches in the ante-

bellum South. By contrast, the North, while a culturally identifiable entity, was not pervasively "the North," but rather, American society. Yet its moral and religious life were increasingly directed away from individualistic religious experience toward public responsibility and social reform.

The North of this era does not present us with any particular surprises, really. Its religious life perpetuated the European, Calvinist, and colonial New England traditions, generally speaking. This means, on the one hand, that the intensity, specifiability, and finality of the conversion experience did not manage a conquest of northern sensibilities and theological understanding which were attuned to the standard three-dimensional approach and the notion that religious knowledge is diffused; on the other hand, that responsibility was construed heavily in social ethical terms. God was viewed as being about the business of bringing the whole world, individuals and society alike, under his government. The reality of the redemption of both arenas called for a complex program of activity to be undertaken concurrently and dialectically.

The irony of the career of southern religion is profound. Its concerns were turned into private ones in order to preserve a public order. And this was as true by action as by reaction. That is to say, the South did more than back away from religious interpretations which would have mandated social reform; it also promoted asocial, individualistic teachings as a kind of quasi-social ethic. By converting individuals, black as well as white, the churches were accomplishing God's will for society, which was thought to consist of two kinds of virtue: personal holiness and the acceptance of one's lot in life. The exemplification of the former would make for a morally pure, upright society; of the latter, for responsibly taking one's place in a divinely ordained order, where black people had their place and whites their various and respective places. Perhaps this hierarchical ordering of people and roles was attributable in part to the English type of society so nearly intactly transported to the southern colonies. It may be that despite the inability of the Church of England to attain wide popular acceptance, it made its indelible mark—aided and abetted of course by the ever more crucial place of slavery and slaves in the society.

The supplanting of Anglicanism by Evangelicalism both accompanied and generated many changes in the society. One of them was its conferring upon the common people a sense of worth and self esteem. Donald Mathews tells us that it enabled them to repudiate the old "class distinctions based on wealth and status . . . with nonclass distinctions based on ideological purity." But he also offers a clue to the later developments under discussion here, namely, that it was *"nonpolitical* in its rejection of political means to attain authenticity and influence."[41] Going farther, the point must be underscored that Evangelicalism's role in uplifting the lower classes was an unintended, adventitious contribution. Its actual program did not include Christian teachings or churchly efforts intended to transform the public realm into the Kingdom of God.

"Ethos without a social ethic." A certain version of our axiom is prominent in Epoch B. We will take a longer look at its pervasive prominence and deeper meaning in the concluding, interpretative chapter. It is enough to say at the moment that the regional church lacked a formulated ethic for addressing its society but that nevertheless it was a powerful influence in uniting the South, calling it to a moral course of action, and legitimating its values. It did not "go public" but it was a public and a publicly signifi-cant institution in the antebellum South. In the sociology of religion's classic terms, it moved from "sect" character-istics to "church" standing. Far from despising "the world" —southern society—and withdrawing from it, the southern churches embraced it, made their identification with it, and sought to direct it in godly paths, in their own special ways, of course.

A religious ideology geared to addressing its social and cultural context is certain to mirror that surrounding context in some ways. Northern religion in Epoch B took the measure of its setting and was shaped thereby, at least partly. Being attuned to the general life of the region, it accommodated itself to the new conditions around it, to the growth of towns and cities, industrialization, the nation's deeply entrenched slavery, immigration with its heterogenizing effect, fresh intellectual currents, oppressive social circumstances for many, and so on. As regards the South, the religious ideology was attuned to its social and cultural context, a fact seen no more clearly than in its bolstering and legitimating slavery. Its posture was to fixate and defend. It fixated and defended the prevailing religious outlook and expected its culture to do the same. South and North, thus, were not merely "near," "close," and diverging, they were also comparable as far as the impact of their religious ideologies was concerned. On the subject of religion narrowly viewed, we may summarize this way: In the South it was fixed and expanding; in the North, it was accommodating and diverse. Each rhythm was consonant with life in its region.

One of the social factors which helped drive the North to a posture of accommodating was the arrival from 1835 forward, for the length of our Epoch B, of a sizeable number of foreign immigrants of alien stock. Ireland and Germany were the European countries adding the largest numbers to the American population in this earliest nineteenth-century wave. Although a few thousand Jews were among those arriving, the great majority was Christian—but these were Christians of different and often objectionable strains. The Germans who were Lutheran caused no great stir by settling in this Anglo-Saxon land, either for themselves or at large; the Germans who were Roman Catholic inflamed more than a few sensitive "pure Americans"; but the coming of Irish Catholics caused widespread consternation. These newcomers were disliked almost as much for being Irish and poor as for being Catholic. But those Americans of Anglo-Saxon stock who reacted to this threat to a stable homogeneity did so indiscriminately. And those whose efforts were being feverishly turned to make this God's nation—that is, Christian, but Protestant, and Anglo-Saxon —resented Roman Catholicism and Roman Catholics of whatever national origin.

Epoch B is the high-water mark of nativist sentiment in the American North. The formation of the Know-Nothing Party stands as the political embodiment of that concern. What interests us here is that ethnic and religious pluralism became a fact of life in the North, resented and resisted by many, to be sure, but a fact of life nevertheless. Of Irish and Germans (with their Catholicism or Lutheranism), American society had known little up to this period. When those had been present, they had either lived quasi-communally, hence away to themselves, or had been assimilated into the wider society, as in the case of colonial English Catholics. Spiritually the North was still Anglo-Saxon Protestant; moreover, the vision of America as properly that kind of nation had never beamed more brightly. But alien peoples and faiths brought alien ways of living. Their presence had to be faced in social attitude and public policy alike. There was to be no turning back of the clock; diversity was to give way to heterogeneity and, in turn, to pluralism.

How dramatically different the southern situation was. Its conception of immigration was limited to the expectation that additional English and Scottish people would be coming, of whom there were few anyway after Independence. Afro-Americans, present by "forced immigration," were not viewed as immigrants at all. With few exceptions the southern population was homogeneous; it was also a homogeneous society. The churches and public policy both were therefore free, as well as obliged, to focus attention on the number one issue: slavery, slaves, and ramifications thereof. It is fascinating to note that an "alien people" determined southern society's course in this period. Yet how different Negro circumstances—and prospects and hopes— were from those surrounding the Irish Catholics of Boston or Philadelphia.

During these years the South labored under a conspiratorial mentality; there is no mistaking that. Insurrections by Negroes, whether actual or prospective, consumed much time in state legislatures even during Epoch A, but especially after Nat Turner fomented his revolution in 1831. All this is well known. Not yet systematically investigated, to my knowledge, is the career of "ism's" in the South. Long before Bolshevism became a regional byword in the 1920s, even earlier than the Civil War, one suspects, Southerners branded a number of ideologies and social movements with the stigma of "ism," among them abolitionism, infidelism, socialism, trade unionism, libertinism, reformism, and modernism. This is an old southern tradition and one to be expected from a "sacred" society, that is, one characterized by a high degree of resistance to change. More precisely, it is "one that elicits from or imparts to its members . . . an unwillingness and/or inability to respond to the culturally new as the new is defined by those members in terms of the society's existing culture."[42]

By and large, organized and strident resistance to change did not surface until the late nineteenth and early twentieth centuries. The Ku Klux Klan is the most infamous of the explicit instances of the South as a "sacred" society, but there have been many more, mostly less institutionalized crusades. The best examples of nativism occurred in Tom Watson's Georgia between 1900 and 1920 and Sidney Catts's Florida late in that span of time. Nativism invaded the main political stream of Deep South life during the first two decades of this century, a half-century and more after it had reared its head in the North. In noting connections like this it is tempting to play the "time lag" game. But to do so with any seriousness is a waste of time because it forces a uniform *chronos* on people, sections, and events. Nevertheless, we should observe how late an abrasive contact with the wider American (and global) society took place in the South. Catholics, Jews, alien ideologies, and strange people with strange-sounding names did not invade the southern consciousness until the twentieth century, or penetrate the actual life of the South with any significant impact until well after World War II.

Doubtless, such developments or their absence contributed much to what was happening in theological circles, North and South, in the years of Epoch B. Once again the differences are very great, even staggering. The intellectual life in the two regions was as "far" and "distant" as can be imagined in a single country with so much "nearness" and "closeness" obtaining in a number of aspects. Social homogeneity in the South and diversity in the North are correlated with the prevailing intellectual life in the two regions, of course, with respect to both cause and effect. European immigrants did not often choose to settle in a social context as far removed from the mainstream as the American South. It featured other liabilities too, like an oppressive climate and a rural economy, but its policies and attitudes as captured by the heading "Old South" sealed its reputation as an unattractive area of residence.

It is the quality of being out of the mainstream which is common to both continuing ethnic homogeneity and a distinctive intellectual life. Avery Craven described this condition among Southerners precisely when he wrote that the "social-intellectual life of the nineteenth century had not come their way."[43] We see this clearly in the status and direction of theological activity in the region. Given the vigor and intensity—even the inventiveness—of southern religious life, we might have expected otherwise. But fixed societies, especially those fixated to place, do not often have the time or perspective for fresh pursuits (as I will discuss further in chapter three). Instead they are busy defending, shoring up, bolstering—the very essence of reactionary behavior. Such is not the soil from which creativity or responsiveness grow.

The state of the antebellum South's theological productivity was of inferior quality, notwithstanding E. Brooks Holifield's recent unearthing of an impressive amount of sophisticated theologizing done by southern clergymen during this period. In his book, *The Southern Theologians: American Theology in Southern Culture, 1795–1860,* a significant theological tradition is brought to light. It was the achievement of town and city ministers; as we shall see, their location and vocations are important.

Holifield introduces us to an "elite hundred" clergymen, Presbyterian (37), Baptist (23), Methodist (18), Episcopalian (14), Lutheran (2), and Roman Catholic (6), who served large and progressive congregations in the larger communities of the Old South. There were doubtless more such "literary parsons," but all of them together made up a small percentage of "preachers" in the South. It is conceivable that 20 percent of the clergymen in the region had been "properly educated" for their vocations. In all likelihood the figure is much smaller; furthermore, many of those who had received education were not truly "properly educated." But some were. Holifield's hundred had been trained at a variety of places, in Europe, at Princeton, Andover, and at a number of other American colleges and seminaries, mostly in the Northeast, but a sizeable minority in the South. "Seventy-three . . . had some college training; nine more received a classical education in private academies; only eighteen were self-educated or instructed solely by private tutors. Thirty-two attended theological seminaries."[44]

Several items in this dimension of southern life are startling. The first is that such a company of well-trained ministers was present on the southern scene. The second is how little impact they actually made; or more accurately stated, how remote they were from the rank and file of the people of the time. Theirs was an elitist, hardly a popular, theology and ministry. Third, these town ministers performed two very different kinds of functions in their formulation and presentation of the Christian message. Their more sophisticated achievements were directed toward apologetics and polemics over against Deism and Unitarianism. These Christian heresies never became powerful in the South but did manage minor beachheads during the teens and twenties of the nineteenth century. Under the real or feared threat of such undesirable teachings, the southern apologists went to work. Their cause was successful, and they doubtless deserve some of the credit for that fact. In addition to that function, they also fed their sheep with practical, vital themes from the Bible and popular Protestant understanding: prayer, pious feelings, introspection, salvation, moral rectitude, sanctification, and so on.

Holifield's cataloguing of the rational enterprises of the gentlemen clergy shows them to be standing in a kind of classical rationalist tradition. In a manner of speaking their thrust was more European than American. Their mentors were the three Johns—Calvin, Locke, and Wesley—of course, but also such philosophical minds as William Paley, David Hume, Immanuel Kant, and Joseph Butler. Some of this was filtered through Americans like Jonathan Edwards, William Ellery Channing, and Nathaniel W. Taylor; but,

as we are about to see, those particular New Englanders'
use of European thought was dominantly practical. What
the sophisticated southern clergymen were imparting to
their congregations in Charleston, Richmond, Savannah,
Danville, Tuscaloosa, and other towns and cities was a rea-
soned defense of and argumentation for the faith. In a
word, they were doing apologetics. Their constituency was
not large. But their perceptions, or predictions, compelled
them to "commend the Christian faith to an expanding
class of educated and aspiring Southerners." Their aim was
to show the "unity of truth and therefore to affirm a 'natural theology' based on human reason as the normal pro-
legomenon, proof, and corollary of Scriptural revelation."[45]
They did so by expatiating on such themes as epistemology,
hermeneutics, the evidences for faith, moral philosophy,
theodicy, biblical criticism, and covenant theology. These
theologians did inhabit the antebellum South; their preach-
ments were heard. Holifield goes on to claim (rightly I
think) that the legacy of their achievements survived the
tumultuous mid- and late-century eras to fuel later liberal
and fundamentalist causes. The fact that both these groups
are minorities in the twentieth century South seems to me
to be of a piece with the role of rationalist thought in Epoch
B. It fell outside the mainstream of regional life and
thought, yet there it was; its reality symbolized a certain
kind and degree of diversity even in a hardening culture.

Among upper-class Southerners there has long been an
affinity to classicism for classicism's sake. The gentlemen
theologians of the Old South were proponents of that point
of view. Their training, love of learning, and perception of
an orderly universe or truth produced a program which
bore directly upon the real world of only a small company
of southern people. The apologetical side of their ministry
did not deliver a "true and lively word" to very many. Yet,
in another sense, their formulations were relevant. Liberal

thought of the Deist and Unitarian varieties had made
some penetration of the South during the century's first
three decades, and was convincing to some down to 1830.
In all probability liberalism would have been squeezed out
in the South anyway, owing to the ever-tightening vise of
evangelical orthodoxy. But some credit for this accomplishment doubtless goes to the effective defense of standard
Christianity thrown up by the gentlemen theologians. Also,
as we have observed, their work did have pertinence to the
better classes of people in many towns and cities.

Further, it provided still another justification of slavery.
Not every last one of the "elite hundred" (and other colleagues) subscribed to the notion of the "spirituality of the
Church" formally advanced by Presbyterian thinkers
(though far more widely accepted); most did, however.
This doctrine, which held that "the Church, as an order of
grace, was permitted no official involvement in the social
reform of the state, an order merely of justice," claimed the
typical southern mind. Holifield's conclusions on the issue
of the relevance of Christian rationalism to the everyday
affairs of southern people square with the central theme of
this study, attention to ethos without an accompanying
social ethic. He writes:

In fact the Southern churches never truly abstained from social
comment; their self-described isolation was merely a protective
gesture during the slavery controversy. Indeed their heavy intellectual investment in moral philosophy ensured that the
gentlemen clergy would continue to address the concrete issues
of Southern society, whether as apologists for existing social
and political arrangements, as unwitting critics of the traditional South, or, on occasion, as cautious spokesmen for human
values.[46]

Meanwhile in the North the vigorous and much-respect-
ed theological tradition launched in the first colonial gen-
erations was flourishing. At Andover, Harvard, Newton,

Yale, and Princeton, along with select pulpits and other theological institutions, a number of front-rank minds were given over to the intellectual formulation of the Christian faith. Some, most notably Charles Hodge and a few others at Princeton, chose the path of defining and elaborating authority, the inerrant teachings of Holy Scripture. Accordingly, their concern was with the eternal message and in that sense, but only in that peculiar sense, with relevance. Either what the Bible taught was relevant, or relevance was an impious delusion. The other two major wings of theological activity were explicitly taken with the salience of relevance; they sought to address the existing and prospective currents of understanding prevalent in a fast-changing society. One of these was composed of the proponents of liberal Christianity, the other made up of those who sought to revise the central stream of northern theology, traditional Calvinism.

We must reiterate that theology in the South and North alike took major bearings from what was happening in the surrounding culture. Yet there were differences between regional developments. In the North there were two classes of theologians, the more philosophically minded ones and those church theologians in divinity schools and pastorates whose most radical activity was to adjust the received tradition. A kind of division of labor prevailed, although most surely not by studied design. Down South the single class of theologians preached from selected pulpits to elitist parishioners. These southern stalwarts were introducing sophisticated theories of truth, knowing, and Christian defense, while also seeking to feed their sheep with daily spiritual bread. Their theological-apologetical labor was largely extraneous to the practical points of doctrine, being more prolegomenological or first-order in nature. By contrast, the goal among the northern church theologians was to transform the preaching from pulpits, the teaching in Sunday

School classes, and the actual engagement of the Christianity of lay people with alternative currents of thought. Their
program was more second-order and practical.

From William Ellery Channing on the conservative end
to Ralph Waldo Emerson on the heretical, the project of
the true liberals was to strip Christianity of its particularist
sting, rendering God accessible to all and no faith scandal-
ous to any. The radicals, or heretical liberals, led by the
Transcendentalists, effectively dismantled Christianity. In
their eyes to do so was a most positive accomplishment inasmuch as it tore down barriers between peoples, exalted
human worth and capacity, and showed men and women
how near the ultimate spirit was for the healing and beauti-
fying of life. The following they attracted was very small.
But the optimism their ideology demonstrated, as well as
the boldness in surrendering traditional religion, was to
enjoy a long life. Extremist as their interpretation was, it
both reflected and directed a major new current of thought
that acquired substantial status in future decades.

Far closer to the received tradition, indeed a quantitative modification of it, was the "New Haven Theology" of
Nathaniel W. Taylor of Yale. A similar assessment applies
to Horace Bushnell, Congregational minister at Hartford.
The paramount issue of this era was human nature: Is it
free? Is it hopelessly contaminated by original sin? Is God
the author of sin? How much moral and spiritual capability
do human beings have? How is divine grace best trans-
mitted to one who has real (if limited) competence to decide to receive that grace for himself? It has been remarked
that the modification of Calvinism was based on the prem-
ise not that God is dead but that man is alive. Taylor,
Bushnell and their theological kinsmen abandoned nothing, transformed nothing—by intention, at any rate.
Caught up in the strong tides of modern psychological
understanding and new drifts in philosophy toward ra-

tionality, they amended, applied, and revised. The emergent intelligence among the young and very bright was finding Calvinism harsh, culpably logical, and negative about human beings. The mainstream northern theology of Epoch B sought to wrest a challenged outlook from an obsolete world-view and to adjust its classical emphases to coincide with the preconceptions of a post-Newtonian era.

Looking back from the vantage-point of the years in the neighborhood of 1980, we are apt to associate the North's revisions of theology with consequences we regard as liberal. What they did help generate was New School thought (among Presbyterians, with analogues in other denominations) and a considerable reforming energy. This took the form of "support for interdenominational evangelistic and reform societies, cooperation with Congregationalists on the frontiers, and a crusade against slavery."[47] We are left with a mixed picture of "liberal" and "conservative." For their own time the liberal revisions were plainly movement against the long-regnant traditionalism. Northern presentations of Christianity, thus, were facing the times and making adjustments in their theology to render it more contemporaneous and more palatable.

We have seen that such southern theology as there was, was worked out by the town and city ministers and was the philosophically rarefied side of their construction, the other side being more conventional and aimed toward nourishing the spirit. It too made a gesture toward relevance, but a relevance geared to the latest European (and Euro-American) rationalistic developments. Rather than being close to the people and the actual situation, it was highfalutin. The southern theology that was preached by the great majority to the largest number was, by contrast, all about the nature (sinful but redeemable) and destiny (in heaven or hell) of all humanity, starting at home. When they wore

their theologian's hats, the gentlemen theologians were
talking about the Christian faith; the real, "sure-'nuff"
Methodist and Baptist preachers were imploring people to
come to a personal faith. Their gentility—in a sense, their
standing above the hurly-burly of ordinary existence—
would seem to be another instance of a tendency toward a
hierarchial society in the South, a tradition carried on in
the "Baptist bourbons" and "high-church Methodists"
down well into the twentieth century. We must not forget,
also, that there was not a separate class of church theologians or philosophical apologists.

South and North, 1835 to 1850, "near" and "close" in a
great many ways, were yet diverging because of different
points of view on slavery, religion, society, and much more.
By 1850 the South had crystallized into a unique culture.
It was not yet a separate nation; it was destined to be that
for only four years, and at that, its political identity was
always something of a sham. The reality under examination then was not political, really, but a "cultural nationalism." Emory Thomas, in a commentary not easily abridged,
fleshes out the contours of that very special social unity
which emerged in our Epoch B.[48] The glue which held it
together, he contends, was religion. "Perhaps Southern
churches are the best place to look for the origins of cultural nationalism in the Old South. There the Southern
mind, conditioned by reverence for the concrete and characterized by assertive individualism, blended with a unique
religious tradition to mold intellectual and cultural life."

Thomas attributes the social and cultural power of religion to several factors. Its homogeneity is a major one; the
presence of a number of statistically minor religious organizations, including Roman Catholics, Jews, Quakers,
and Unitarians hardly made a dent in the solid wall of
mainline Protestantism. The transdenominational popu-

larity of revivals and camp meetings, plus the "ease and
frequency with which Southerners attended services of various denominations" attest to the prevailing homogeneity.

Widely shared theological convictions played their part
as well. The belief that human beings are profoundly sin-
ful lay at the heart of this near uniformity of belief. That
dark assessment was somewhat relieved by the promise of
perfection in the life to come. But its reality was underscored in an inverse fashion by the "hedonistic aspects of
the Southern lifestyle." Indeed it did manifest a great deal
of "sloth and lust," as Northern critics charged, and a great
fondness for drinking hard liquor. Thomas concludes that
"hedonism and fundamentalism coexisted in the Southern
soul," making confession, purgation, and going out to sin
some more all a part of the southern religious scene. Yet
nothing about this scene invited an optimistic interpretation of human nature or capacity. Southerners, upper-class
and lower-class alike, Episcopalians and Baptists both, "perceived reality as rooted in human frailty, and because they
could not alter the human condition, they accepted and
even celebrated their humanity."

In his researches into the role of religion during the Confederate era, Thomas notes the persistence of the familiar
pattern in the relation of ethos and social ethic. The accepted theology sanctioned the regional status quo, most
notably on the issue of slavery. However, it did promote
change—*repentance* is the term so often used but so rarely
manifested in southern society.

Southern Protestantism made severe demands upon Southerners as individuals; the common conviction called upon
them to live upright lives in response to the righteous demands
of a strict father-God, and, whether they were obedient or re-
bellious children, they acknowledged the existence of individual moral obligations. About society, however, Southern Protestantism had much less to say. Religion in the South was

essentially personal; it did not, as elsewhere, inspire, reform or create in believers a zeal to perfect human society. Southerners believed in the power of Protestant Christianity to regenerate individuals, but when the church entered the arena of social justice, it had "quit preaching and begun meddling."

When you have a powerful social unit which is not formally a political state, something must hold it together. At the level of public issue, slavery served that function. At the level of spirit or soul, evangelical religion provided the cement. The years before the Civil War were in many ways religion's halcyon days; yet in other ways they were its darkest hours. Whatever one's interpretation, the Old South and the Confederate States of America could not have existed without the popular religion of the region.

THREE

Strangers in the Same Household
1885–1900

Touching on South and North in American religion in
the years around 1900, the historian Vann Woodward
noted significant regional religious differences.

> Upon good authority one learns that there were three tenden-
> cies "clearly discernible" in American Christianity of this pe-
> riod: "a trend toward church unity, a further liberalizing of
> theology and an increasing emphasis upon socialized religion."
> Yet one searches vainly for important manifestations of any
> one of these three tendencies in the annals of Southern Chris-
> tendom. Instead, there is evidence that the current in the
> South ran counter to all three tendencies.[1]

This perceptive passage stands as a kind of text on which
to build the analysis of our Epoch C, the last fifteen years
of the nineteenth century. Generally speaking, things were
as Woodward describes them. Our diachronic and more
specialized approach here, however, should open up wider
and better-defined vistas for viewing conditions in religion
and society during this period.

We may begin at the conclusion, by observing that the
South as stereotyped by outsiders and as the embodiment
of feelings of inferiority, antagonism, and insulation is a
development of the half-century following the Civil War
rather than the one leading up to it. The "New South"
period witnessed the real flowering of the region's famous
identity, although of course its taproot lay deeply em-

bedded in the soil of the Old South. This fact is substantiated by David Potter in the course of his denial that there
was a "deeply felt southern nationalism" during the years
of the "impending crisis" just before the Civil War. There
was such a thing, he contends, but later. It "resulted from
the shared sacrifices, the shared efforts, and the shared de-
feat (which is often more unifying than victory) of the
Civil War. The Civil War did far more to produce a southern nationalism which flourished in the cult of the Lost
Cause than southern nationalism did to produce the war."[2]
Furthermore, this negative southern outlook did not reach
its full development until after the Reconstruction era had
ended (in 1877). Our Epoch C is the period of the ripening
of these attitudes of "inferiority, antagonism, and insulation" within the mind of the South and its attendant reputation beyond. The symbolic fruit of this evolution was the
spate of Jim Crow legislation enacted and enforced in the
southern states. Vying successfully for the title of cultural
cement, however, is religion.[3] In many ways this period
represents the beginning of southern religion as we think
of it today. The South was as solid religiously as in any
other aspect, with perhaps party politics being its only
formidable rival.

We have seen that in Epoch A religion was somewhat
"fluid and unpredictable" in a sort of preformed state south
of the Mason-Dixon line and "changing and mobile" while
given direction and anchorage north of it. In Epoch B the
southern pattern was set and expanding, fixed and defensive; by contrast the northern was accommodating and
diverse. Now, in the latest of our three periods, it had come
to be set and exclusive in the South, while divided and even
amorphous in the North. Northern religion had never been
so unanchored, so lacking in discernible direction. Indeed,
there was no such identifiable thing as "northern religion,"
not even with reference to a prevailing norm; there were

only patterns to be traced, piecemeal, giving shape to an inordinately complex religious situation. Down South homogeneity and centripetality were characteristic, also stronger than ever, and were accompanied by a massive penetration of uniform thinking and social obligation. It did follow, although not especially for logical reasons, that South and North were "far" and "distant," strangers to each other, despite their being bound by a common destiny within a single nation.

In his 1966 Lamar Lectures, Clement Eaton contended that while the Old South civilization was most assuredly waning in the two decades following the close of the Civil War, the "diapason of life had not changed" by 1880 or even 1890. Apart from slavery, the passing of which was regretted by few Southerners, the South "remained strongly attached to the values and philosophy of the Old South." Despite the tragedies and vicissitudes of that tumultuous era," much of the Old South survived, waning very gradually."[4] The progressive Southerner Walter Hines Page identified three ghosts from the past that haunted the southern mind through our Epoch C and even into the early years of the new century: the cult of the lost cause, that is, the admiration of Confederate times and leaders; "the fear that underlay the dogma of white supremacy"; and "the ghost of religious orthodoxy."[5] The contemporaneous Page and our contemporary Eaton are pointing to the continuity between the assertive South of the antebellum and politically separatist years, on the one hand, and the decades before and after 1900, on the other. Southern culture was retrenching—some would say ossifying—and religion was both an aspect of and a contributor to that conservatism.

The force of this state of affairs is only seen for all its significance when one trains the other eye on a northern society vibrant with adjustments to what may be called, almost literally, a new world. Robert Wiebe refers to the

North of this era as a "distended society," meaning one splintering into a welter of contending factions and increasingly marked by cultural diversity.[6] While the historians offer slightly varying interpretations as to the precisely critical watershed, all agree that the 1880s and 1890s were transitional, either as watershed or as the period of the "old" society's demise before the "new" society's taking form in the 1920s.

Demographic circumstances were being radically revised by the arrival of massive numbers of immigrants, the "flood tide" hitting American shores between 1880 and 1914. Moreover these were a culturally alien people, different in language, customs, religion, politics, and habits from the settled majority. On another front, northern life was shifting from a dominant base in small and large towns and rural areas to city-life as industrialization became characteristic of so much of the North's economy, its features and problems becoming an ingredient in values and policies affecting midwestern farmers as well as New England factory workers. The mention of one other stark trait of northern life will suffice to register the severe contrast between the two regions, namely, the incursion of modern intellectualism into the North. This produced a severe ideological disruption. All three disparities had the most direct bearing on the comparative religious situations, the last only the most obviously. South and North were, indeed, "distant" during this period. But the truth of the matter is even more dramatic than that; the North's time of most extensive "challenge and response" was the South's era of greatest defensiveness and ingrowth. A salient illustration of this turns up inadvertently in a recent chronicling of American history, *The Great·Republic*, by five major historians. In the entire length of this large volume's Part 5, dealing with "nationalizing the Public" (by John L. Thomas), only a few short paragraphs treat the economic

and political South. Any charges of regional bias or of cul-
pable oversight are unfounded, really; what is at issue is the
sociocultural divergence of the South from the North—
actually from its own nation—and from practice and
thought in the western world at large. What studies of this
period in American history tell us in this regard is that the
issues and problems addressed by the federal government
are the North's, not the South's. Nearly all the major developments in the "modernization" of America were associated with the North. The South's history had brought it
to a position of standing outside—if also inevitably along-
side—the modern climate of opinion and peculiarly modern activities and attitudes.

In a manner of speaking, the old southern rallying cry
of "state's rights" (at least, the principle thereof) had become informally more operative than it ever had managed
to be as a formal political position in the Old South. A passage from Woodward summarizes this divergence of
"strangers in the same household" quite well:

The year 1877 marked the end of a period of social, economic,
and political revolution in the South. This revolution had as
one of its avowed aims the ending of the "house divided," and
as the objective of a secondary phase of coercive reorganization
the removal of such remaining differences as set Southern society apart. The end result, however, was actually to widen
and deepen the disparity between the revolutionized society
and the rest of the Union in several important respects, particularly those of wealth, living standard, and general welfare.[7]

It would be easy to demarcate the regional distinctions
so vividly as to conceal the similarities and points of contact. They were, after all, parts of the same nation, with a
shared political and economic system, and both were inevitably involved in all processes engulfing the entirety of
western society. (The same had been true ever since the
nation's beginnings as the furious struggle over slavery it-

self attests.) Concretely, the South did participate in the industrial and economic changes which were rearranging life so significantly in the North and in Europe. Through the founding or enlarging of such industries as textiles, iron and steel, tobacco, and lumber, and the opening of hundreds of miles of railroad lines, the South underwent what Woodward calls an "industrial evolution." It lagged behind, but its condition was hardly inert. Even in this connection, however, we must recall that a great deal of the capital for southern investment and expansion flowed from the North and from Europe. Financiers like Plant, Morgan, Gould, Depew, Disston, and Knapp hardly belonged to the best families of the South. Moreover, a majority of southern employees were still agricultural laborers; this was true even in those states where the textile industry had grown impressively. Victor S. Clark could thus conclude in 1909 that "the South was and continues to be mainly an agricultural region" and that it has "not in this respect, followed the example of Great Britain and New England."[8] Nevertheless, it was "progressing" toward greater economic diversity; nothing else was possible, given its ineluctable participation in the affairs of modern western states.

Southern optimism and boosterism aside, the big news in the region was—still—race. Afro-Americans made up a far larger portion of the population than minority groups usually do, the percentage standing at just about 30 throughout Epoch C (and changing very little until after 1910). There were some 5,962,000 Negroes in the region in 1880 and 7,550,600 by 1900. These numbers and proportions alone had much to do with the racial question's remaining the preoccupying energy within the dominating white population. Negroes were here, there, and everywhere. Their residence—and citizenship—in the South was as solidly established as anyone else's. Their presence and their finally indisputable humanity occasioned the making of many decisions and regulations. It is true, as someone has remarked, that the South has squandered an enormous amount of psychic energy on this anachronism; it was an anachronism in wider western civilization from at least the 1830s. But it was doing so with all deliberate vigor in our Epoch C, in fact, along certain lines as never before.

Emancipation had been declared in 1862. The Reconstruction of the southern states lasted from the war down to 1877. It was an experiment bent, among other things, on the implementation of the Negroes' freedom, hitherto merely a legal fiction. Despite these and other efforts in behalf of Negro rights and opportunities, it was difficult to observe a practical distinction between old slave and new nigger. In some ways, southern blacks had known a better lot before freedom than state legislatures built for them in the 1880s and 1890s. (The abrogation of slavery was of course an immense step forward which would eventually result in the granting of rights and opportunities to these American citizens.)

The Jim Crow story is too familiar to require any detailed treatment here. It should be remembered that public opinion about what was desirable, necessary, and providentially justified, namely, social codes, preceded the laws embodying those values; but no less important is their transformation into laws. The separation of the races in railroad cars, streetcars, public schools, parks, theaters, hotels, courts, libraries, residential districts, cemeteries, sidewalks, and so on, was enacted into law principally in the 1880s. Paradoxically this was the same era when white democratic movements were wresting control from the Redeemers. The Black Codes of 1865–1866 had gone to no such complex lengths to define Negro identity and delineate Negroes' behavior. Yet by 1900 things had grown worse still, as white people assumed an ever more pessimistic and negative—sometimes violent—attitude toward their black fellow residents. The caste system encouraged fewer constructive qualities than slavery had. Woodward summarizes the situation in this passage:

Upon one opinion both whites and blacks, Northerners and Southerners appeared to be in agreement—that the transition from the slavery system to the caste system had been accomplished at the cost of grave deterioration in race relations. The intimacy of contact under slavery, especially that between the better type of both races, was succeeded by a harsh and rigid separation. Under slavery, as W. E. B. DuBois, for example, pointed out, the two races sometimes "lived in the same house, shared in the family life, often attended the same church, and talked and conversed with each other," while under the caste system there was "little or no intellectual commerce" between races. "Ours is a world of inexorable divisions," wrote [Edgar Gardner] Murphy. Segregation had "made of our eating and drinking, our buying and selling, our labor and housing, our rents, our railroads, our orphanages and prisons, our recreations, our very institutions of religion, a problem of race as well as a problem of maintenance." [9]

The disfranchisement of Negroes from the 1890s was consistent with the segregation policies just enumerated and served to seal their fate. Virtually no opportunities existed for Negroes, economically, educationally, or humanly in general; and all political routes to altering that drastic human condition were cut off by the varieties of legislation enacted in the 1890s.

Meanwhile, we must ask, what was happening in the religious spheres of southern life? Among the Negro population, Christianity was flourishing. It had become a meaningful world view, and one widely shared, during the last three decades of slavery. The facts of its attractiveness and effectiveness under the social conditions of that period tend to amaze later observers looking back. It turned out to be consolation and mainstay. More than that, in the antebellum period the white evangelical message that the lost and condemned required conversion for pardon and eternal rewards was standard fare, both in the Negroes' own services and in the churches they attended that were led altogether by whites in the white manner. Later observers looking back also have difficulty grasping the powerful appeal of a message about sin and salvation to a people confined to a living hell here and now. All that is important to say is that it did. We know this from records dating from that period.[10]

But we see the real importance of religion most impressively in the zeal with which southern Negroes, once they were freed and the war was over, claimed religion as their own special, independent provenance. Within weeks of the war's close, Negro congregations were being organized. As this movement spread, the tendency toward forming separate denominations accelerated. In Kenneth Bailey's words, "What had begun as a local shuffling into all-white and all-Negro congregations . . . developed into denominational separatism."[11] Concurrently the theology of the black people's Christianity was shifting, not away from glorious heaven, to be sure, but away from the threats of hell. It remained a religion of salvation, but less and less from eternal punishment and more from alienation from Jesus, who sweetens life, offers, hope, gives strength, loves each for what he or she is, confers dignity and worth, binds people together, commands righteous living, and—bless the Lord—takes the faithful up to live with him for ever and ever.

Negro Christians could make their theology their own because their churches were their own. Within the South's second largest body, "the colored Methodists were leaving almost *en masse* for the Northern Church or for the African bodies."[12] The African Methodist Episcopal Church had been organized in Philadelphia in 1816 and the A. M. E.,

Zion, Church five years later. Not particularly popular in the Old South, these bodies became viable alternatives to the Methodist Episcopal Church, South, once freedom had been declared. A comparable indigenous development culminated with the organization of the Colored Methodist Episcopal Church in America in Jackson, Tennessee, in 1870. The Eleventh Census reveals these significant statistics for 1890. In the Methodist Episcopal Church, South, the traditional white denomination, Negro membership stood at 242,926. Within several African Methodist bodies (proliferation had produced eight by this date), the total was 854,200. Thus, nearly 1.1 million Negro Methodists were recorded as church members a quarter-century after the war. This reflects enormous growth from the reported 209,836 figures of Negro membership in the Methodist Episcopal Church, South, in 1861 (even when the likely imprecision of all such accountings is allowed for).[13]

Christianity, largely alien to black experience in the colonial period and more a world-view than a basis for community in the antebellum decades, had become the predominant form of institutional life for southern blacks in the late nineteenth century. Baptist statistics point this up even more dramatically. There appear to have been some 400,000 Baptists in 1860. The Eleventh Census shows 1,348,989 Baptists. (Few of these belonged to the Southern Baptist Convention. The Sunday School Board of the Southern Baptist Convention officially excluded Negro congregations from its statistical reports for the first time in 1872.)[14] This large company was divided between the National Baptist Convention, Negro Baptists' first national body, founded in 1895 as the amalgamation of three separate bodies, and a nonideological independency. Northern Baptists (white) were quite active in a variety of ministries to southern Negroes, some educational, some welfare-related, others directly ecclesiastical, but they did not specialize in incorporating southern Negroes into churches affiliated with their northern white denomination.

The southern black population had been resoundingly Christianized by Epoch C. While it was true that many still did not hold church membership, very few were ignorant of or alienated from the Euro-American religious tradition as that had been adapted to Afro-American circumstances by this time. The Baptist and Methodist denominations had become the largest affiliations by far, with the Presbyterian, Roman Catholic, Episcopal, and emerging sectarian communions attracting small followings. The Baptists and Methodists were reaping the harvest they had sown in the stressful years of the Old South. These, after all, were the familiar forms of religion; already Negro identification with them was strong. From 1865 forward they were destined to be representative of the religious life of the emancipated people. The churches' roles became even more powerful than that, however; they were the social center, educational agency, political platform, and heart of the black community. The reason for such comprehensive success is that the churches stood as the one unit where the Negroes' experience and social toleration by the ruling whites were combined. Negroes knew what the church was all about and how to give impetus to its ongoing life. It was theirs; they had been vital participants in it for a long time.[15] Additionally, they knew little of any other social institution, such as political parties, farmers' granges, commercial business, schools, and the like, at first hand; political developments of the 1880s and 1890s did little to enhance their familiarity with any of those publicly oriented agencies of society, to say the least. If rural southern whites could enumerate "the home, the school, and the church" as the fundamental units of society, blacks could point merely to the home and the church, with only the latter requiring institutionalization and affording any kind of public purchase. The church thus became *the* institution in the black community, and the ministry the single occupation (and sole profession) to which aspiring men could turn. What the church did for and meant to a quasi-free, oppressed minority was of enormous magnitude, both personally and socially. What black people did by way of revising Christianity is also immense in range and impressive in quality. They adapted it to their own experience and the limits of their opportunity; in the process, they created an authentic folk variant of a traditional religion. It featured expressiveness, joy, fellowship, moral responsibility, pious feelings, and the hope of heaven. It deemphasized guilt and punishment, ecclesiastical forms, and learning. While denominational affiliation made for some differences, it is fitting to speak, as several have done, of black Christianity as a unique "denomination" of that religion as forged in the crucible of its unique history.

That is one chapter in the religious life of the southern population during Epoch C. But it is part of a larger, longer narrative. Whites had introduced blacks to Christianity. Blacks had gone on to create their own version of Christianity, however, informally in the Old South days and now in formal institutions. The fact that they did so was grounded in their relation to the white majority. Yet, paradoxically, it also furthered their segregation from the higher caste. In no small part, this was due to the distinctiveness of their folk version of religion. The essential withdrawal of white Baptists from the affairs of their Negro brethren was another factor. Methodists of the two races remained somewhat more closely in touch, as befits the Methodist sense of churchmanship. In the final analysis, however, whites generally backed off from involvement with blacks to the same degree as blacks, determined to manage their own religious affairs, turned away from whites. In both negative and positive respects the Baptist role was the largest and most characteristic.

The Southern Baptist Convention began the postwar period with acknowledgments of "special obligations to the Negro." Even at this stage, however, as John Eighmy puts it, "systematic efforts to facilitate the freedmen's religious reconstruction were almost negligible."[16] With the passing of the next couple of decades, stated obligation and organized efforts diverged even more sharply. Work among the Negroes was "never altogether lacking," but little of consequence was begun and less endured. This is not to say, however, that the Southern Baptists departed from the white cultural norm in overlooking or outflanking the dominating racial factor in southern society. Eighmy notes the extensive awareness by white Baptists of the blacks' socially deprived condition as reflected in nearly all denominational conventions and often in the press. The "real significance of the attention Southern Baptists gave" to black people, he suggests, "lies in their awareness of the problems confronting blacks and their chronic failure to contribute substantially toward improving those conditions." The conclusion he reaches is consistent with his thesis that the Southern Baptists have been in "cultural captivity": "As for the unwillingness of white Baptists to support any effective program to uplift blacks socially, the best answer seems to be that any such effort would have run against the mainstream of contemporary Southern policy."[17]

We have previously noted that Baptists of the South were less closely in touch with their northern brethren than were the southern Methodists, and that this was related to the difference between localist and connectionalist notions of the church. Given this state of affairs, a Methodist concern for reunion was far likelier to be kept alive; the reconstruction of a national Methodist Church did occur in 1939. There has not been any serious and widespread interest

among Baptists in the South to join forces with their northern coreligionists. (Nor is there any evidence that such interest is apt to be kindled.) Nevertheless, in certain peculiar
and ironic ways, Baptists were "nearer" each other across
regional lines than Methodists. That phenomenon constitutes quite a story.

Baptist historian Robert Baker highlights the troublesome but determined activities of the Southern Baptist
Convention to "establish a geographical base." That was an
issue because of the divergent northern and southern Baptist views on denominational organization, symbolized by
the terms *society* in use in the North and *board* in the
South. *Society* referred to a benevolent organization, one
for home missions, another for foreign missions, a third for
publications, and so on, each of which had a single function
and the confederation of which was characterized more by
each unit's independence than by centralization. In Baker's
words, each society "functioned for one benevolence only,
minimized geography and denominational unity in favor
of widespread financial support, and ignored all other
denominational emphases as being the province of other
societies." It follows from this ideology that the Home Mission Society of New York (northern Baptist) considered
itself perfectly free to carry on its ministry anywhere a perceived need existed, including the southern states. By
contrast, the Southern Convention "desired a geographical-
ly-based denominational body that would assume leadership in all of the benevolences the constituency might
desire to cultivate."

Given these disparate organizational strategies, friction
was inevitable. It did so at the point of the Home Mission
Society's presence in the older southern states and, as well,
in Missouri and the territories of Oklahoma and New
Mexico. The society's investment and involvement down
South were not small. In 1882, for example, the society had

"67 missionaries in 13 states of the South in their evangelistic program, 13 schools with 78 teachers and 2,329 pupils
(principally Negro) in the South, and had provided extensive assistance to churches of all races in the construct-
ing of church buildings." Contacts then were pervasive and
persistent, if not numerous. The Southern Convention's
response to this took firm and forceful shape in the 1880s,
with the result that before 1900 northern Baptist influence
in the South was neutralized by being confined to certain
schools and colleges for Negroes and Indians.[18]

On the positive side, the growth of the benevolent agencies of the Southern Convention during the 1890s and
thereafter was enormous. If the spiritual destiny of the
Southern Baptist Convention was outlined in the fifteen
years before the Civil War, it achieved concrete form in
Epoch C (and definitive position in the 1920s), hence our
earlier contention that "in certain peculiar and ironic
ways" the Baptists of the South and the North had never
been "nearer" than in the last years of the nineteenth
century. The fact that "nearness" was at such odds with
"closeness," however, meant the cessation of significant constructive interaction between the two major white Baptist
bodies, a condition which lasts until this day.

We must be quite clear, though, that animosity is not
what primarily characterized the relationship then, nor
most certainly does it now; rather, the Southern Convention's all-dominating self-containedness was the primary
feature of its "foreign policy." It set its course toward living
unto itself, committed to being faithful to its own standards
and vision. Then and now, its posture is more accurately
depicted as nonecumenical than antiecumenical, as non-
cooperative rather than uncooperative. I believe Baker puts
his finger on this attitude emergent during Epoch C by
linking the Southern Baptist Convention's mentality with
that of the South in general:

The South had always had a distinctive sectional cohesiveness. Social, economic, political, and linguistic patterns of slavery after 1619 accentuated this sectional uniqueness. The struggles for religious liberty and the union of Regular and Separate Baptists brought a sense of southern unity. The strong blows of Primitivism and Campbellism severely affected Southern Baptists before their organization in 1845 and instilled a battle-field type of solidarity. The events of 1861 to 1877 deepened the southern sectional feelings.[19]

This heritage was only tightened by developments of the years before and after 1900, all of which focused on the question of "loyalty to the Convention."

Virtually all historians of the period are agreed that the severe and bitter sectionalist spirit had waned greatly by the 1890s. Southern people and their leaders alike were ready to acknowledge that the reunion of 1865 was a solid and lasting political fact and that Southerners and Northerners were such by virtue of being Americans first. The Spanish-American War, a milestone of reconciliation, objectified this growing awareness of national unity by presenting the whole nation with a cause. Soldiers from both sides of the Mason and Dixon line fought to curb Spain's power in various island nations and to extend the American empire. In a certain real sense the South was reincorporated into the national society, especially politically, during the 1890s.

Culturally, however, the South remained sectionalist, by choice, by dint of memory, and by virtue of public circumstances. This was the era, after all, of the organization of the United Confederate Veterans, the United Daughters of the Confederacy, and the United Sons of the Confederacy. Let us remember that it was also the period of Jim Crow laws which epitomized the retention, even the elaboration, of traditional regional racial values. In religion, too, we see another stark example of continuing Southernness. Most obviously, Baptists, Methodists, and Presbyterians remained regionally organized. That, according to Paul Buck, is to understate the case. He concludes "that the churches remained sectional bodies, an antagonistic element in the integration of national life." One aspect of this was the "sorry spectacle of clergymen standing as the most radical of sectionalists."[20]

More subtly, southern Christians became forthright in claims to the superiority of their region's version(s) of Christianity. Addresses to denominational assemblies, editorials in church papers, and sermons are full of comparative references, always to the South's advantage, of course. (The propensity to compare may be more telling than the substance of the comparisons.) Erosion of pure, traditional Christianity in the North and in Europe was noted and lamented, seemingly even gloried in; it was attributed to the inroads of various "ism's," among them evolutionism, theological liberalism, and a cooling of evangelical ardor, but not excluding Roman Catholicism and Judaism, the respective faiths of millions of new immigrants. In the South, by contrast, the orthodox faith was proceeding virtually unchallenged, and most certainly without adulteration. As Bailey states the case: "A preoccupation with individual repentance, a dogged insistence on Biblical inerrancy, a tendency toward overt expression of intense religious emotions: these legacies of frontier revivalism still held a primacy."[21] Its influence had never been greater, its ministers never more respected, and its hold on the southern mind remarkably fast. The hope of the world lay in Christianity's message, the South declaimed, and its purest proclaimers anywhere were the devout Protestants of the American South.[22] A sense of regional religious destiny was emerging which was to arrive at an advanced stage of development in the years surrounding World War I.

This self-consciousness and high self-esteem is transparently a product of southern society in these years of recu-

peration from the ravages of war and reconciliation with
the nation at large. That spirit showed up in a number of
ways. One was the spurning of the North's self-regard as
the more characteristically American of the two regions;
the South preferred viewing itself as a unit within a larger
unit.[23] A second was the inclination to compare itself with
the North, a factor already noted. Third, the restriction
of the categories of analysis to the South's frame of reference tells us a great deal about life in the region during this
period. Fourth, the emergent sense of destiny shows us how
"cosmopolitan" the South was, in certain peculiar respects.
It did not want to interact with the wider world on any
terms other than its own; but it also was much too much a
part of the larger world to ignore all the rest (the "nearness" factor again). Accordingly, it did think to compare.
More importantly for our purposes, the regional denominations embarked on vigorous home and foreign missions
enterprises. Perhaps there are few better confirmations of
the validity of Frederick Jackson Turner's "frontier hy-
pothesis" than the zeal of the southern churches to expand
their horizons just as the American frontier was closing,
about 1890. While they could not look northward, they
could look westward and beyond the national boundaries.
One gains the impression that they were doing more, certainly not less, than responding to Christ's Great Commission; they may also have needed something big to do, a
challenging task, a way out of their insulation, such as that
provided by China, India, Korea, Latin peoples at home
and abroad, and American Indians. But, conjectures aside,
the world of their demographic recognition far exceeded
the limits of the regional culture with which they were so
satisfied and which they defended so fervently.

   In his study of three nineteenth-century American missionaries in East Shantung, entitled *Their Ordered Lives
Confess*, Irwin T. Hyatt suggests some interpretations of

the enormous impact of the famous Lottie Moon on Southern Baptist life. Miss Charlotte Moon was born "with a silver spoon in her mouth" in Virginia in 1840, and was well educated and widely experienced. Serving as a missionary from her southern denomination from 1873 until her death in 1912, she performed heroic service against great odds. In terms of statistical successes, her achievements were not particularly notable; over all, however, her career was most impressive. In consequence, her name was seized by the Women's Missionary Union of the Southern Baptist Convention for its annual Christmas foreign missions offering in 1918. The magnitude of the donations received since then is astronomical, now approaching forty million dollars each year. Why has the story of this one woman (the romanticization of which does not detract from the genuine impressiveness of her life) captured the imagination of the nation's largest Protestant denomination with such a staggering effect?

Hyatt draws upon Leslie Fiedler's idealized love theme as one suggestive explanation. "The kind of life involved here . . . is interracial. It is idealized because it represents an 'exploration of responsibility and failure,' or vicarious atonement for white racial crimes at home; it is also idealized because 'to develop it openly would unleash the twin taboos of homosexuality and miscegenation.' " Like model lovers in the novels of Melville and Dana,

all become wanderers, that is, and find love and forgiveness in some exotic place, with a non-white race more palatable than the people sinned against at home. Such lovers also choose partners of their own sex and love them chastely, thereby conveying an impression more acceptable than the thought of any kind of interracial male-female affection.

A comparable analysis of Lottie Moon's career and the phenomenon of the Lottie Moon Christmas Offering is provided by Lillian Smith, the southern novelist. As

Hyatt tells it, "She sees the traditional religious activism of southern Protestant white women in terms of race-associated sexual frustrations. Their missionary enthusiasm she views as an escape from facing wrongs nearer at hand, and as a perversion on several levels of what she thinks love ought to be." Finally, in a passage of measured but pointed reference to the South's inability to take to its own heart the message it so exulted in transmitting to the heathen, Hyatt waxes prophetic:

The Dear 'Old Southland—so traditionally talented at helping people like Lottie Moon receive calls elsewhere—has represented her as a personification of its traditional norms. None of the lessons that the "best educated woman in Virginia" learned at such painful cost over so many years in China, lessons about humility and sympathy, and imitating Christ, emerge at all. Her P'ingtu experience and her mature idea of human community—her conviction that she, the Chinese, and the folks back home were equally brothers and sisters—have been discussed mostly in terms of her own suffering, of a gifted daughter dying in some faraway place. And very little has been said about what she was taught by those dull people whose Christlike example she aspired to be.[24]

Whatever else may be said about the southern churches in our Epoch C, one comprehensive feature of their career in those years was their vigor and aggressiveness. Desultory and lackluster though much about southern life in this period may seem to have been, the churches were busy. Impelled by many forces, the most intentionalist of which was to "preach the gospel to all, . . . making disciples," their growth in numbers of members, in elaboration of organized life, in variety of tasks envisioned and undertaken, and in permeation of southern society and culture was truly remarkable. We have noted something of their organizational expansion and missionary enterprise. Throughout, their impact on life in the South has been implied; it is encapsulated in Farish's summation that "during those years religion played a dominant role in the life of the Southern people." In support, he quotes the opinion of Methodist Bishop Atticus G. Haygood in 1880, that since the Civil War, the "controlling sentiment of the Southern people in city and hamlet, in camp and field, among white and black has been religious." As time went on, this was to become even truer.[25]

The sheer magnitude of numerical growth within the homeland tells its own story. As Woodward observes, "instead of withering away before the advance of industry, science, and urbanization, the Southern legions of Christian soldiers multiplied in numbers and, to judge from appearance, waxed in zeal."[26] *The Bureau of the Census: Religious Bodies* for 1906 shows an increase in church membership to 9,260,899 from the 1890 total of 6,139,023. What is even more noteworthy, though, is that the increase in church membership outdistanced population growth by 12 points, 51 percent to 39 percent. A huge proportion of increase in both membership totals and rate of growth occurred among Baptists and Methodists. Roman Catholic ranks were swelling enormously in the North, but that church's strength down South was confined to the traditional areas of Louisiana, Kentucky, and Maryland. The 1906 religious census disclosed a Protestant hegemony unbelievable for a pluralistic nation. In the South, east of the Mississippi River and excepting only Kentucky, 96.6 percent of the church members were Protestant, with nine out of ten of this company belonging to either Methodist or Baptist churches. The greatest growth was in those two traditions, spread through several types and formal organizations of each, the Baptists especially. Within our period, however, there also came into being offshoots of Wesleyan pietism, which became new sects. Among these were the Pentecostal Holiness Church, the Church of God, and the Church of the Nazarene. This upsurge of simple, highly expressive, vital piety was part of a national movement late in the last and early in the present century. But the South generated its own indigenous forms, which were to be part of the panoply of Protestant bodies to be taken seriously as permanent, influential presences in the region. While they typically attracted the lower classes of people and were most often found in rural, mountain, and industrial communities, they became an essential element in the southern scene.

One of the emergent indigenous sects stood out from the rest in several important respects. The Churches of Christ were first enumerated as such in the 1906 census of religious bodies, but their profile had been apparent for a half-century by then. (Now, as then, they are not a denomination, but a movement or brotherhood composed of independent congregations owning no responsibility to anything beyond themselves.) The seeds for their growth and eventual formation had been planted by the Campbellite tradition, the Disciples of Christ, whose theological founder was Alexander Campbell. With roots tracing back to 1804 or so, the "Christian Church" was solidly established by 1830. The decade of the fifties witnessed a separation, indeed an alienation, between the mid-South Campbellites and those firmly planted in Kentucky and from there north and west. The 1906 census disclosed a membership of 156,658, nearly all of it in the South or border states. The figures were 101,734 in the eleven states of the old Confederacy and an additional 30,206 in Kentucky, West Virginia, Missouri, and Oklahoma.

Reference has been made to the distinctiveness of this movement from the variety of pietistic sects which were born around 1900. For one thing, its areas of original strength soon became specifiable, middle and west Tennessee and nothern Alabama being the strongholds. As the population grew on the far side of the Mississippi, the brotherhood developed strength in certain areas of Texas, Arkansas, and Oklahoma. In the second place, where it was strong, it appealed to the solid citizens of the community, making substantial gains among the middle classes. It had begun as a company of the southern poor, but gradually evolved into a position of strength, where it competed with the major denominations for members and standing. Charles A. Scarboro's research reveals that the Churches of Christ were "sectarian," that is, opposed to the "Southern regional establishment," but at the same time they maintained a "churchly," that is, a "supportive relationship to the plain-folk of the transmontane mid-South." This brotherhood served as an ethnic or quasi-ethnic community for its members and simultaneously stood at variance from American national society and culture.[27]

Thirdly, it was a rationalist tradition, which located it in a different camp from the pietism of both the new sects and the old denominations. Its champions were debaters who could better their adversaries in theological argument, proving that theirs was *the* New Testament church. How different this was from the value-system of the other communions; there, effectiveness in winning souls for Christ and power in testifying to God's direct action in one's soul (and body), were regarded as the authentic manifestations of true religion. This southern Campbellite tradition defies all general, usual, and typical social scientific accountings for distinctive southern folk religion. But it has been there from the 1850s, in strength since before 1900, and it "fits" in the regional scene. Its reality reminds us that rationalism and scholasticism too—not only Evangelicalism—are ingredients in the southern religious experience.

Still other fin de siècle cracks in the solid evangelical walls were located in the mainline denominations themselves. Carrying the metaphor a step further, these threatened to weaken the foundations of the structure. I refer to the dismissals of faculty members adjudged theological heretics from institutions supported by the major denominations. At Vanderbilt University in Nashville, at Columbia Seminary in South Carolina, and at Southern Baptist Seminary in Louisville, pressure was mounted which resulted in the pressured or forced departure of distinguished scholars. Two of the four most celebrated cases took place before 1885, but all reflect the religious situation of the South in Epoch C. The evangelical religion had spread wide, and the reign of orthodoxy had been firmly established. To Bailey's mind, what the ouster of the four professors points to was the "degree of consensus on such issues." [28] The North, too, knew of heresy trials and firings, but nothing of the degree of consensus that distinguished the South.

We are seeing that for all its "farness" and "distantness," actually its cultural insulation, the South was not impervious to the "acids of modernity." South and North in this period were indeed members of, if also stronger in, the same household. C. H. Toy, a Virginia Baptist trained in the critical methods of Old Testament scholarship in Germany, was pressured from his Baptist seminary professorship of ten years tenure because of his espousal of views unacceptable to the conservative biblicism of his sponsoring denomination. (Toy's career bears out the marvels of southern history: He had once been engaged to marry Miss Lottie Moon; and following his dismissal from a regional seminary he was appointed to a professorship at Harvard.) Alexander Winchell, the Vanderbilt geologist, ran into a Methodist buzz-saw over his application of Darwinian theory to the Genesis account of the creation of man; his part-time lectureship at Vanderbilt was terminated in 1878. Historical accuracy requires mention that these two ousters were rather gentle and patient in manner. The firing of James Woodrow by the Presbyterians from the faculty of

their Columbia Seminary was more acerbic. An uncle of
Woodrow Wilson, Woodrow, too, was Germany-trained
and had been an officer in the Confederate army. Despite excellent credentials as a scholar he was dismissed
in 1886, also because of his evolutionary theory in interpretation of the Bible. Darwin and Genesis were the focal
points of southern orthodoxy's fears; any blows struck at
man's uniqueness and direct divine creation were repelled
χas attacks on the evangelical doctrine of salvation. If there
were no human beings to be saved, the Savior came for
naught.

The other celebrated firing of this era involved William
H. Whitsitt of the Baptists' Louisville seminary; the year
was 1898. The sin for which he paid a price did not have to
do with fundamental Christian questions such as biblical
interpretation, creation, sin, or salvation, but with sectarian
concerns. A church historian (also trained in Germany),
Whitsitt denied that the Baptist tradition could be traced
back any earlier than 1611 and, what was far more damag-
ing, that the first generation of Baptists in England practiced baptism by "sprinkling," not immersion. In presenting
these fruits of his historical research, Whitsitt ran afoul
of a current in Southern Baptist life called Landmarkism
which contended (in a manner not unlike the Churches of
Christ) that the local Baptist church was the only true
church, there being an unbroken connection of Baptist
churches through the centuries back to the apostolic age.
He also was advocating, or at least so it seemed to his constituency, liberalism and "German rationalism." At the
deepest level, his principal error was to threaten a denominational unity—which was "prized above all other consid-
erations," according to Eighmy—and a yearning by the
Southern Baptists to achieve the clearest possible "identity
as a separate religious body." [29]

The battle over the Bible generated more fireworks than

putative sectarian erosions and was a far more widely recognized problem. Yet both tell us quite a lot about the
southern religious outlook in Epoch C. The first attests to
the tenacity of theological orthodoxy and to the South's
satisfaction with what it had. Its commitment to the Bible
symbolized, fostered, and legitimized the region's self-
assurance about its course; there was scant interest in sacred
scripture's prophetic edge. It had little to learn from alien
schools of thought, not even through dialogue as a forum.
I have argued elsewhere that the sense of southern self-
satisfaction militated against consideration of alternative
theological points of view. To have entertained them seriously might have called into question the intimate alliance
between religion and culture that the region had been
working out for more than half a century. A viable equi-
poise had been achieved. Accordingly, the South did not
want its prospective ministers going North for their theological education, nor its educators coming back home to
teach via the groves of academe in Europe or New England.
The second, the Baptists' ethnocentrism (which the Presbyterians came close to matching), is a transparent part of
the need for belonging to a subsociety that is cohesive,
right, and possessed of destiny. Such identification occasioned more than a few sparks in arguments over "which
party is right"—an old American concern—within the
region itself, but more than that, it equipped them with a
conviction of "being somebody" at a time when neither the
South's accomplishments nor its reputation in the rest of
the western world offered much reassurance.

The South's reputation beyond its own borders was indeed sullied. This was due in large part to its historic and
continuing defense of Negro subjugation and to its backwardness in economic and educational matters. But the
eye of the beholder also contributed to its low esteem. In
the North, life was bustling, forging ahead; Epoch C was

an era of vast changes and dramatically fresh circumstances there. That part of the country had good reason to consider itself to be representative America, on the wave of the future, in touch with the vital developments of a forward-looking age. The South was stagnant in the backwaters; the North, by sharpest contrast, was progressing across the waters of an exciting, recently entered ocean. Caught up in the same tides of liberal optimism (in religious terms, secularized eschatology) as western Europe, that part of America could tolerate and manage its enormous social problems because it believed them to be soluble, even the means to the realization of a new age. New wealth, new powers of government, new peoples, new industrial achievements, a new American empire, new means of travel and communications, new philosophies of meaning and practice—everything seemed new, liberated from the shackles of tradition and opened to vast opportunities in the future. What had been the rhetoric of hope in colonial and early national times now seemed practically realizable.

The day-to-day life of both ordinary people and leaders of society in the American North between 1885 and 1900 hardly squared with any such glowing description, however. Governmental and other public activities had seldom been more demanding; corruption in financial and political life, the emergence of powerful monopolies, and the arrival of millions of aliens, among other problems, produced a turbulent public setting. As far as the ordinary people were concerned, well, many of them were recent immigrants for whom life was often an economic, linguistic, and cultural nightmare. Many others were the victims of the new wealth through expanded industry. Continually struggling with poverty and deprived of their rights, they were virtually powerless. A sharp disparity prevailed between the spirit of the age and the rigors of life in a revolutionized society. But that spirit was abroad; it affected most sectors of life, not least those immigrants who were as sorely victimized as anyone.

Consider the differences between South and North in this regard. One way to study them is through a typology I have formulated around the correlation of space and time; the ideal types are "moving time" and "fixed time," "moving space" and "fixed space." When applied to the values of a society they are meant to suggest profiles of conservatism and liberalism, or closedness and openness to change. I believe we may properly and helpfully describe northern society in Epoch C as oriented to "moving time." This is the most liberal, most open to change, of the four. It is a mentality that lives by the conviction that things are progressing, that change is both fact of life and a highly positive value. By sharpest contrast, the South of this era was a "fixed space" society, the most conservative of the four societal styles. When such a generalized attitude prevails, values are linked to a particular place irrespective of history. What happens in that space serves as a framework of identity and of the true. This is indeed a more conservative—less open, less dialogic, more closed, fixed, and reassured—outlook on reality. Carl Degler reaches a related conclusion (from different perspectives of analysis) in his study of southern distinctiveness suggestively entitled *Place over Time*. A central part, the subjective dimension, of his definition of the South is that the "people who live there . . . recognize their kinship with one another and, by the same token, those who live outside the South . . . recognize that southerners are somehow different from them." Degler concludes that this has been true since the colonial period and is still true; accordingly it is the place that makes the difference, pretty much irrespective of when one lives there. (The period of history does make a quantitative difference, of course, both in Degler's analysis and my own interpretation.)[30]

While the North was being transformed into a remarkably new society, with all the strains and hopefulness that attend such a heady outlook, the South was ever more turned in on itself, sequestered, defensive, ideological, insulated, and given to advertising its own superiority. This was the situation despite the impossibility of isolation; insulated it was but scarcely isolated. The two regions were strangers to each other but unmistakably bonded together in the same household. In a very real sense the importance of the South's distinctiveness consisted entirely in its being part of a larger societal unit. Religiously, its life was characterized as set, dominant, and exclusive. Simultaneously, northern religion was divided, shifting, tending toward formlessness. Religious patterns and theological currents underwent radical transformation in this period, chiefly in response to social novelties and dislocations.

Most obviously the Protestant dominance of society from New England to the West was confronting a severe challenge. In certain respects this was nothing new; already the Roman Catholic church had become the nation's largest religious body in the 1840s. But its impact in the middle decades of the century was minimal and its people socially marginal. We should also bear in mind that World War II, John Kennedy's election as president in 1960, and the civil rights revolution of the 1960s was the complex of events which brought the entire nation to a frank acknowledgment of its fundamental pluralism. Notwithstanding these historical observations, the North yielded its pervasively Protestant character during Epoch C. Virtually every county in the heartland of classical Puritanism now counted a Catholic majority. Similarly, in nearly every large northern city, from New York and Philadelphia to Cleveland and Chicago, the Catholic population surpassed the Protestant. The settlement of Jewish immigrants in selected, mostly urban locations, further altered the complexion of religious patterns in the North. Thus, what had early been a Protestant nation in fact and intention, and later in desire if not in deed, had been forced to share its position of legitimacy and even strength with a historically unwanted and feared version of Christianity and the one sizeable company of people in Western civilization who have stood outside Christianity altogether.

The modulation of diversity toward pluralism, a condition defined by the philosophy that all human beings have equal claim to standing within the society, is bound to make impact on the traditional religion of a society. The religion can no longer confidently proclaim its metaphysical truth or its status as society's moral foundation and very soul; because these claims are relaxed, an entire world-view is called into question, then shattered. A commitment to religious parsimony, more often simply taken for granted than understood and contended for, is severely tested by the emergence of a social pluralism, that is, the sheer fact of a variety of groups, each claiming to be authentic and protected by law in the promotion of such a view.

After a while, the presence of a social diversity raises questions about theoretical pluralism. Conservative groups (which are reactionary) and the traditionally dominant groups both have a problem in accepting any such departure from their respective norms. The conservatives essentially ignore the diversity, retreating from a diverse society to a haven within which they claim an exclusive religious purity. The traditionally dominant group is forced to come face to face with the new society in the nature of the case; it resents its loss of exclusive high standing and is more apt to fight its battles over that cause than over religious pluralism. Some such scenario does seem to have characterized the socioreligious adjustments of western societies in the wake of the Enlightenment and the process of democratization. In the American North the Protestant ruling classes

regretted their loss of standing and resented the outlanders
who were depriving them of it. As time went on, they adjusted to this as a fact of life, knowing in what directions
the laws and conventions of the nation pointed. Their religious adjustments as such came more easily. Doubtless
some of the conservatives knowingly thought that such liberalism was poorly equipped for curbing any tendency to
surrender the timeless faith. At any rate, the northern
conservatives resisted the adulteration of the faith by tightening traditional forms or inventing new forms of traditionalism thought to be an improvement on the existing
earthen vessels; in fact, they attempted a recovery of the
simple, primitive faith. The "Princeton theology" exem-
plifies that sector within northern conservatism which
tightened traditional forms, and the rise of modern Fundamentalism epitomizes the spirit of reactionary conservatism.

In these two major ways, the former by far the more
prominent in Epoch C, the religion of the North was a response to dramatically new circumstances. Before glancing
at each of these in turn, we should note the rather aston-
ishing fact that neither held any particular charm for
southern Christians. It was predictable that the South
would have no truck with the traditionalism of the ruling
classes and their greater friendliness to theological adjustments, which were branded as liberalism and openness to
"German rationalism." Surprisingly, they were almost as
little attracted by the conservative reactions. Genuine
Fundamentalism remained largely a northern phenomenon. Much of this is explained by the relative, though far
from total, paucity of contacts and by the South's preoccupation with itself and its regional institutions. At the same
time, the northern conservatism was simply of a different
sort from the South's. It was more similar and attractive to
theoretical Presbyterianism than to the Baptist and Methodist faith and people, but it scored few successes any-

where. One is finally driven to the conclusion that southern conservatism was as much southern as conservative; that is, the South generated its own kind of conservatism. Substantively speaking, it was more sensitive to piety and dedicated to the evangelization of lost souls than authority-minded or given over to the preservation of pure Christianity understood rationalistically. To this day, incidentally, the northern public is puzzled by, and often wrong in its assessments of popular southern religion, tending to judge it by its own significantly different standards of measurement.

In his description of the Third Great Awakening in American Christianity from 1890 to 1920, McLoughlin makes no mention of the South. In the context of his analysis, the reason is the absence of a general, identifiable awakening during the period. Perhaps we may say no revival of religion occurred in the land of revivals during Epoch C and just beyond, although burgeoning church growth and rampant revivalism pervaded the South. In fact, it was the era of the regularization of revivalism. In other words, an "Awakening" occurred in a northern society alternately religiously dormant and beset by threatening new forces, while the southern society fastened itself ever more firmly onto a form of religion basically characterized by revivalism. It was the standard fare of many churches and a common occurrence in most others.

Even "modern revivalism," the highly organized, professionalized kind so common in the North since Charles G. Finney and the 1830s, was relatively insignificant in the South during the last years of the century. The famous northern evangelist Dwight L. Moody conducted only a few campaigns in Dixie. One Southerner, Sam P. Jones of Georgia, was ubiquitous and effective enough to be dubbed "the Moody of the South." During the years of his public career, which peaked in the late 1880s, he covered the southland, and even made a few forays into the North. Yet

the mark he made was much smaller than those made by
his counterparts in the North, because of the particular
role of revivalistic religion in the culture. Additionally,
his enterprise gradually shifted away from the norms and
conventions of revivalistic preaching toward right conduct.
"He wanted deeds, not words, as the test of salvation." To
produce cataclysmic conversion experiences was not the
goal of his work; his aim was to rid the South of strong
drink, gambling, the "continental sabbath," and other
moral evils.[31] Thus the presence of a Sam Jones does not
alter the basic conclusion that the Third Great Awakening
was overwhelmingly a northern phenomenon.

Northern theology itself then tended to go in one of two
major directions. One branch took no decisive notice of
changes taking place in the culture (except by reaction),
because to have done so, in the phraseology of a later generation, would have amounted to letting the world set the
agenda for the church. The other branch engaged those
changes and sought ways of reformulating its belief and
ministry that were congruent with new discoveries in science, sociology, psychology, textual study, and the like.
The latter approach became mainstream northern religion,
of course. It won quite a following within the erstwhile
sectlike Methodist and Baptist denominations, and in doc-
trinally tough-minded Presbyterianism, as well as in those
northern denominations which played minor roles through
their southern kinsmen, such as Congregationalism and
Lutheranism.

The baptizing of the spirit of the age showed up in several ways, the most important of which were an ecumenical
attitude, critical study of the biblical documents, and the
rise of the Social Gospel. The first came to formal maturity
somewhat later than our period, in 1908, with the organization of the Federal Council of Churches and then of
the International Missionary Council of 1910. Well before

the turn of the century, however, a strong trend toward ecumenism had been developing, as exhibited by the popularity of the Y.M.C.A. and Y.W.C.A., and the formation of the Student Volunteer Movement for Foreign Missions in 1888. Cultural factors had a great deal to do with this, needless to say. One was the perceived need for protestant Christians to band together in the face of Catholicism's rising numbers and dominance; a formidable rival (enemy?) can best be dealt with by a united army, after all. Another was the emerging strength of theological liberalism, resulting in the departicularization of denominational theology and getting its strength from the overweening importance attached to reformulating Christianity in contemporary terms for the benefit of a society flirting with secularism, irrespective of confessional niceties. (It should be pointed out too that the ecumenical impetus had had a long history in the North. Congregationalists and Presbyterians had often been close and cooperative from the eighteenth century. Revivalism, in the North especially, had been fostering the minimizing of a party spirit along theological lines from the heyday of Charles G. Finney in the 1820s.)

Methods of biblical interpretation also were a truly major and representative change in northern religious life. The subjection of the text of the Bible to scientific analysis, the same kinds of analysis as any other text from the ancient (or modern, for that matter) world, had reached an advanced stage in Europe by the 1860s and was beginning to become prominent in America. We have noted that Southerners C. H. Toy and James Woodrow had studied in Germany, where the critical methods of the study of the Bible had become their own. Northern scholarship was more broadly exposed to these currents of thought not only because the lure of training abroad was greater and its pursuit more acceptable, but also because several American graduate schools were founded on the German model: Johns Hopkins, Yale, Harvard, Columbia, and, in the 1890s, the University of Chicago. Moreover, an additional factor played on the American scene, rendering the new criticism even more attractive and tightening its hold, namely, the spirit of "social Darwinism." To archeology, the study of ancient languages, textual criticism, historical research, and related fields of inquiry the Americans added, with special relish, the evolutionary factor so consistent with prevailing societal notions of progress. It should be re-marked that biblical criticism generally, and the evolution-ary factor specifically, were hardly new and most certainly not uniquely northern. But during our Epoch C this way of understanding Christianity's sacred scriptures became standard fare in the major seminaries of the mainline de-nominations, including the Baptist and Methodist. A few heads rolled even so, and some conservative seminaries were founded in reaction. Moreover, resistance to this putative threat to the classic faith was considerable among the rank-and-file church members and the conservatives (usually fundamentalist). But there was no turning back the clock.

The South, on the other hand, simply lived in a different theological time-zone. The inroads that were being made into the establishment of regional theological seminaries in this period were expressed quietly and held cautiously. Among the church people such novelties were rarely heard, owing to the clergy's reluctance to embrace, or at least openly declare, a conversion to the new thought. Such in-timations of revolutionized approaches to the Christian authority rarely met with any acceptance. But it is im-portant to see the real differences between South and North, which boil down to the impenetrability of southern culture on account of its enshrined values. And this was true despite the existence of currents of thought within the culture that would have created dialogue, at the very least.

Liberal thought was about, especially in colleges (less so in seminaries), and among Methodists more than among the salvation-minded Baptists and rationalist Presbyterians. Randolph-Macon, Wofford, and the auspiciously begun Vanderbilt were in touch with the wider educational scene in part because there were professors on their faculties trained in the Germanic tradition, whether abroad or north of Washington. Methodism's open stance is captured in these words of Farish's:

Aside from the fact that Southern Methodism continued to entertain a traditional Protestant hostility to the "fatal errors" of Catholicism which encouraged a spirit of intolerance and bigotry where that faith was concerned, the absence of particularistic doctrines and exclusive pretensions served to make its adherents tolerant of other creeds. Moreover, their active cooperation with other denominations inclined them to liberality in doctrinal matters, making them the more ready to examine critically their own creed.[32]

The evidence suggests that such attitudes came somewhat closer to the life of the people than the sophisticated interpretations offered by the "gentlemen theologians" of the antebellum period. Yet what is truly startling about these streams of liberal thought was how little impact they did make.

A recurring theme throughout our diachronic examination of American religion has been the ongoing diversification in the religious patterns of the North since its beginnings in a tradition of solid convictions, paralleled by the South's gradual codification of an originally loose tradition. The late years of the nineteenth century represent the apex of that codification. A few alien winds were blowing against the southern walls and some blew down wooden parapets atop them. But the walls stood firm, as did the well-anchored articles on top and inside. Regional insulation, aberrant racial attitudes, economic backwardness, and religious orthodoxy were among those features which were changed very little, remaining constant until many decades later. Most assuredly, the South of Epoch C was not a monolithic society. Yet there were social and cultural norms implanted deep in the region's people. Subtle, insinuating change could be attempted and not infrequently realized; openly to challenge well-entrenched norms was to flirt with or even invite the annihilation of the tendered position. By contrast, the North's normativity was collapsing near century's end, making for greater ease of penetration. By way of capping this interpretation, I suggest that the South's diversity was far greater than its homogeneity indicated, but that it had little effect since the whole was unequal to the sum of its parts.

The Social Gospel, its presence or absence, and its nature, is the final item in this theological series requiring attention. What the term refers to is a conviction that the Christian God cares as much for the larger context of living, the economic, political, physical, and all the other suprapersonal elements of mankind's life, as for the personal or spiritual dimensions of an individual's existence. Accordingly, the reign of God over the public and secular spheres, through the application of the values and concerns associated with his will for the world, is as basic as the salvation of lost souls, the upholding of the authority of the Bible, and the cultivation of warm, personal piety. In other words, the Lord's will for the world is comprehensive and constructive, including things as well as people, matter as well as spirit, public as well as private, secular as well as sacred, structures as well as personalities. When viewed in that theoretical light, the so-called Social Gospel does not seem so strange or deviant. After all, the South's founding Christian tradition, the Church of England, functioned with some such notion of its responsibility, heavily conditioned of course by its unique history in the old country and the peculiar social circumstances of the colonies. To an even greater degree, northern religious life, from its beginnings as a Calvinist colony impelled by the mandate to create a holy commonwealth, had viewed its task in such an all-encompassing framework. When the stir which the emergence of the Social Gospel created (or represented) is looked at against the backdrop of *early* American history, one wonders briefly, why the stir, and what occasioned it?

The period of infancy and childhood does not a personality make, at least not in the career of a society. In the South, an inclination to choose between evangelism and social ministries was apparent in the upsurge of the Methodist and Baptist causes in the later eighteenth and early nineteenth centuries. What was anticipated through those developments had acquired full growth by 1820 or so. In his study of the relation between "revivals" and "awakenings" on one side and "reform" on the other, McLoughlin illuminates the absence of a linkage in the South during the Second Great Awakening (1800–1830):

The reason why southern revivalism failed to produce the same kind of political reform and institutional restructuring that occurred among "romantic perfectionists" in the North lies in the problem of slavery. Even a major prophet like Peter Cartwright dared not touch on the issue of slavery in his sermons after 1830, and when he tried in other ways to oppose that institution, he was finally forced to give up preaching in the South. He was not afraid to say that slavery was "a domestic, political, and moral evil," but southern folk were unwilling to hear it. The mixing of social reform and spiritual affairs cut too deeply into the traditional fabric of the southern way of life. It threatened rather than consolidated communities; it promised violence when the function of religion was to curtail violence.[33]

This spirit, quite generally applied, was summarized in doctrine of the "spirituality of the church" which was spelled out by James Henley Thornwell for the Presbyterian majority in the 1850s, though it already enjoyed effective if unformulated currency among the three largest denominations. Ernest Trice Thompson records for us a representative application of this doctrine, given in 1887 by the Reverend A. B. Curry of Darien, Georgia, in connection with the one issue, as we shall see, on which many southern churches were to act in Social Gospel fashion:

Mr. Curry contended that the church, as such, was not free to espouse the prohibition cause, or any similar enterprise, or to league itself to it in any way whatever. "The Church," he insisted, "is a Kingdom whose laws are all made for her by her King. The code is placed in her hand, finished and complete in every respect. No power is given to her to alter this code." Since prohibition is not inculcated in the Bible, it follows, as night follows day, that no such political solution may be espoused by a church, whose ends are spiritual, and whose power is spiritual. Is the church then to stand aloof? By no means, responded Mr. Curry. Let it preach temperance as a spiritual grace, drunkenness as a spiritual evil, teach this with authority, and enforce it when necessary through the divine power of the keys. "This is the Church's way of dealing with the Temperance question. It stands in favorable contrast to Prohibition."[34]

The South's origins in Anglicanism and its ironic preoccupation with ethos notwithstanding, its dominant religious bodies had repudiated anything resembling a social interpretation of the gospel well before the Civil War. The pressures of the late-century years further hardened that position. Accordingly, a major Methodist spokesman could declare that the "peculiar mission of the Methodist Episcopal Church, South, is that it alone stands for the Christian principle of staying out of politics."[35] Their view became one, not of tolerating a social interpretation, but of repudiating it as a denial of Christian faithfulness and of rejecting those who practiced such falsehood.

The North had its own problems with the Social Gospel

construction of Christian responsibility. To all intents and purposes, northern Protestantism divided into two parties in the generation following the Civil War. In another context we had occasion earlier to note this development, referring to the two wings then simply as "traditionalist" (or mainline) and "conservative" (or fundamentalist). A more precise designation is suggested in this context, namely, the public and private parties.[36] For the northern mainline, the public party in Protestantism, Christians' and the churches' primary tasks addressed the health of life in a society beset by such myriad changes as industrialization, urbanization, new ways of thinking, and the dramatic alteration in demographic patterns. What actually happened is that most leaders in the public party gave their primary attention to this kind of ministry. In most instances, church people in that company had not espoused subjectively oriented means to incorporating new members since before the Civil War. Thus the converting of those outside the fold and the dramatic rejuvenation of the indifferent baptized was deemphasized; passions, strategies, and notoriety were given over to Social Gospel causes. Incidentally, a representative short list of those causes looks like this: equal rights, abolition of child labor, prevention of poverty, arbitration of labor disputes, a six-day work week, and a living wage.

The instincts of the private party pushed in different directions. They saw their commission hardly at all in "both-and" terms (sacred and secular, spiritual and physical, etc.); it is more accurate to say that they were characterized less by single-mindedness than by the rejection of a second set of tasks. Their vocation was to stand firm on the Word of God. That kind of thinking is as much concerned with the "that" as with the "what," with authority-mindedness as with what exactly the authoritative text says. Purity, thus, was a supreme value. The private party abstained from entangling alliance with the world and from any complicity with man-made theories. It thus minded its own biblical, spiritual business. It was private by definition inasmuch as it saw its mission as the promotion of the church's life in and of itself, not as an institution called upon to bear prophetic witness to the society at large in the interest of reform. In another way, too, it was private: it refused to have anything to do with other brands of Christians, sometimes resorting to attacks on their infidelity, but most of the time simply avoiding any fellowship with them. That knife cut both ways, however, since the public party was typically just as uninterested in joining hands in a common task. Snobbery and disdain prevailed in both camps, their exact expressions taking shapes appropriate to the respective mentalities.

Social Gospel developments thus turned out to be divisive between the regions and within the North. One is impressed by the relative absence of party conflict around this issue inside the South. Isolated individuals and small organizations, a decade or two later than Epoch C, for the most part, did appear on the scene to do battle with the South's versions of similar conditions eliciting activity among northern churchmen. Nor were the denominations totally unaware of the need to address certain cancerous problems in southern society. Yet by no stretch of the imagination can it be said that a strong Social Gospel tradition lived as an element in regional religious life. Two corollaries must be entered here in order to disclose the complexity of the situation. The first is that northern Social Gospellers were about as insensitive to racial injustices and consequent need for reform as southern Christians were. Their focus was trained almost everywhere else, it seems, but they were blind to the need for applying Christian values to the plight of Negroes in both regions, including the huge numbers who were to move toward northern jobs and greater personal freedom in the first two decades of the twentieth century. (The blindness was greater, however, before than after the turn of the century.)

The second corollary has to do with alcoholic beverages—their manufacture, sale, and consumption. Contrary to popular assumptions, the use and abuse of alcohol, not only the obviously social and structural problems for which it is famous, were planks in the (northern) Social Gospel platform. Furthermore, the cause for Temperance (a euphemism for total abstinence) was waged far more vigorously in the North than the South, down to the 1880s at any rate. What is curious, and significant, about regional responses to the alcoholic beverage issue is that during Epoch C, a time when the number of "dry" states in the North was approaching zero and the cause was being laid to rest, it was becoming ever more popular in the South. Joseph Gusfield offers an interpretation of the earlier strength and later decline of this "symbolic crusade":

Drinking has been one of the significant consumption habits distinguishing one subculture from another. . . . The rural, native American Protestant of the nineteenth century respected Temperance ideals. He adhered to a culture in which self-control, industriousness, and impulse renunciation were both praised and made necessary. . . . In the twentieth century this is less often true. As Americans are less work-minded, more urban, and less theological, the same behavior which once brought rewards and self-assurance to the abstainer today more often brings contempt and rejection. . . . Abstinence has lost much of its utility to confer prestige and esteem.[37]

If we take Gusfield's analysis as a device for understanding the Temperance reform movements, we note, first, how culturally similar South and North were at least through the antebellum decades, really down to the 1880s. We must also note the difference he draws between native Protestants, on the one hand, and all sorts of immigrants, Protestant as well as Catholic and Jewish, on the other. The South's being for the most part untouched by immigration, therefore, bulks large as a distinguishing factor.[38] But at least one other congeries of factors contributed to the South's retention of the older northern tradition—not really its own—at the time when its grip on northern society was being relaxed. It was somehow tied in with southern guilt, defensiveness, insulation, and claims to ideological, moral, and religious superiority. In turn that entire complex of attitudes was linked to the racial policies and values of southern society. One is not quite sure how to finger the decisive factors. These offer themselves as explanation: (1) the need for a scapegoat to account for the South's lot; (2) the use of liquor seen as a threat to the stability of home and family, the region's dominant social institution; (3) the fact that liquor's being a great equalizer might facilitate black people and white people becoming too familiar with each other; (4) similarly, alcohol's use as a crutch for facing up to guilt and inferiority and for adulterating the impact of fate; (5) likewise, the denominations' need for badges of identity, taking up this cause and outdoing each other in advancing it.

Arriving at an altogether satisfactory explanation as to why the South became so adamant in its moral opposition to liquor and so vigorous in its crusades to rid society of it is problem-ridden at best. What is clear is that where there is that much smoke, some fire must be raging out of control. Also, we know that the crusade against the "liquor traffic" in all its aspects became a preoccupation and, in effect, popular southern Protestantism's version of the Social Gospel. That is to say, churches that had abstained from political activity for reasons of conviction plunged into the fray on this issue. The Baptists, who adhered to separation of church and state principles, threw theory to the wind in this case, so definitively did they identify liquor as the prime moral evil.[39] Presbyterians in 1887 considered traveling the same route, but the doctrine of the "spirituality of the church" prevented them from direct political activity such as the endorsement of the prohibition movement.[40] Nevertheless these two denominations, and their Methodist brethren as well, influenced public opinion and political policies in behalf of this cause. The Methodist Episcopal Church, South, made its position unequivocal in legislation adopted at the 1890 General Conference in St. Louis: "We are emphatically a prohibition church. . . . We offer no compromise to and seek no terms for a sin of this heinous quality. We are opposed to all forms of license of this iniquity."[41]

Woodward and his "good authority" were right. Strictly in churchly or theological terms, what was happening in the North, in Protestantism at any rate, consisted of "a trend toward church unity, a further liberalizing of theology, and an increasing emphasis upon socialized religion." It is also correct that down South none of these tendencies was much in evidence, and, in fact, that "the current in the South ran counter to all three tendencies." Of course the matter is more complex than that, as we have begun to note; also there are deeper layers and other kinds of factors which help describe and account for the differences.

As much as any single factor, the homogeneity of the South's society and the high degree of its consensus on numerous major values and concerns are what distinguished it from a northern society wherein "social-structural differentiation" was already taking place. There are few better clues than that device of the social sciences for clarifying the differences between South and North at the end of the nineteenth century. Social-structural differentiation had begun to characterize northern society; it was not to do so in the South until well after World War II. It is a process in which

institutions are pulled out of the close articulation that char- acterizes the undifferentiated community. Politics, education, the family, the economy, and even religion become more spe- cialized and more autonomous. The possibility of one domi- nating another grows more remote as each becomes an island unto itself. Each institution is likely to have more contact with its national affiliates than with different institutions in the same community.[42]

In the South of Epoch C "modern" society had not yet come into being. The various aspects of life, private and public, in their formal and informal institutional expres- sions, had not yet been made complex. All were seen to overlap. One could dominate another, or many others. Re- ligiously speaking, it was still conceivable that the church could hold all the others together and penetrate each with its values. The favorite southern phrase, "Christ should dominate every area of life," reflects not only a theological commission but also a sociological possibility—for an ear- lier time, that is. Dominating the values by which the peo- ple lived as the church did, it had no need to infiltrate the structures that constitute so much of life in society. As they became more reified and far more complex, its previously effective strategy—a fact which may have contributed to its disinterest in the Social Gospel—grew obsolete. Its per- meation of the world-view and value-system of individuals continued; any desire it ever entertained to redeem social structures packed steadily smaller potential. In the nature of the case, the mainline northern church came to grips with this societal occurrence: Its theology had to pick and choose between personal and impersonal ministries, to some degree at least; its ministers often found it advisable to select a specialized vocation, comprehensive ministries becoming more and more difficult to carry out effectively. The divergent possibilities with reference to the churches' influence on the various cities of mankind's life are transparent to the "farness" and "distantness" of South and North between 1885 and 1900. The two regional cultures had finally reaped the history of their actual but insignificant colonial distinctiveness and their abrasive antebellum distinctiveness. What is curious is that this happened at a time when both ineluctably belonged to the same nation, society, and basic culture, so that their distinctiveness by 1980 has become increasingly limited and mostly a colorful fact of history.

Conclusion

DRAWING COMPARISONS AND CONTRASTS BETWEEN THE RE-
ligious life of the two historic cultural regions of the United
States has proven to be a king-sized and risk-filled undertaking. Even so, that venture can be better realized for past
periods than for our contemporary times. American society
has not been so subject to homogenization or a national
cultural unity ever before in its history; only the colonial
period begins to compare.

We have had occasion to observe the extent of interaction between the South and the North in three key periods, 1795–1810, 1835–1850, and 1885–1900, determining
whether the two regions have lived near to or far from
each other. Similarly we have examined how close or distant the culture of the two peoples has been in those epochs.
In summary, the succession through the three epochs has
been something like this: (1) culturally, the movement was
from notable differences in A to distinctiveness in B, to divergence in C; (2) interaction between them ranged from
small and growing in A to much in B, to limited extent in
C; (3) interdependence was minor in A, greatly present in
B, and considerably diminished in C; (4) the tone of interregional relations moved from life apart in A, toward dis-
engagement in B, to deep-seated animosity in C.

A glance at the application of those questions to contemporary America is particularly fruitful, as we are about
to see. But it is well to sketch the barest outline of the role

of religion in the South in the three periods first, to form a kind of grid made up of regional correlation and the comparative place of religion. During Epoch A religion was conservative early and innovative late. The progression was from keeping European traditions alive and reinforcing class-structure toward fostering social change. During 1835–1850 religion conserved; it set the limits of change and legitimized consensual values. Epoch C was religion's reactionary era in the South; it was used to preserve and sanctify the reigning ethic. The northern progression was from an entrenched normativity in A, to an internal revisionism during B, and the dissolution of the region's religious tradition in favor of radical pluralism in C.

In the years around 1980 the grid of forces operating in the South shows significant change from the situation around 1900, while conditions in the North are only a more intensified version of those prevailing at the turn of the century. This dramatic shift in the situation of the contemporary South has, in fact, brought life in the two regions toward greater commonality. As for cultural correlation, the differences are no longer noticeable. Interaction between the two regions is now very great, in practically all respects. Interdependence is so extensive that its existence is taken for granted. The tone of interregional relations is better than good; it amounts to life together.

If it was important to rehearse the impingement of the past upon the present, it is imperative to see the cultural and social unity—not to say uniformity—of the present through the dramatic contrasts between our time and earlier times. (In actuality we mean from the beginning, though more sharply from 1790 or so, all the way down to the 1960s.) The recentness of the informal and structural, that is, cultural and social coming together of the South and the North can hardly be overstressed; moreover, the coming together is profound in its depth and almost certain to be permanent. The kind of diachronic approach pursued in this analysis highlights the drama of interregional relationships. In a nutshell we have seen them to move from an intimate parallelism to a distinct parallelism and divergence, to a kind of cultural perpendicularity, and now to a parallelism approaching congruity, the differences being insignificant societally, and no greater than interesting, culturally.

The South remains an identifiable cultural region (many subregions in one, of course); no North, as such, has existed for nearly a century. In Dixie, regional dialects, culinary tastes, styles of community life, interracial relations, and, not least, religious patterns still show a distinctiveness, sometimes bordering on a kind of quaintness, that reflects its peculiar history. And the persistence of regional "religious patterns" reflects more than demographic and geographical conditions. A few illustrations will have to suffice to make the point.

1. Evangelical Protestantism is a family of Christianity present in North and South alike. Any list of its adherents includes the Baptist, Nazarene, Pentecostal, Assemblies and Churches of God, and Holiness bodies (though not all members of each, especially in the case of the first). But many others in the so-called mainline denominations, in small free church groups, among a variety of Calvinist descendants, and elsewhere warrant the evangelical classification. With respect to most of these examples, differences are slight between the regions. It is startlingly true, however, that the majority of southern Evangelicals are piety-minded and aggressively evangelistic, while the largest number of such Christians in the North are authority-minded and moderate in intensity of outreach. Both companies live under a sense of urgency, are very clear on their identity, are deeply convinced as to the authenticity of their beliefs, and are self-consciously devout. Styles diverge

though at the point of central task: southern Evangelicals are more single-minded in being dominantly evangelistic, putting the salvation of souls as first priority; their northern counterparts are tougher, less aggressive, more demanding, and, often, more given to social responsibility.

2. The contrast between northern and southern religion in our era is seen clearly when one asks whether a regional religious consensus prevails. Northern society has no religious normativity; certain sections are dominated by one tradition—those are not numerous or large—but even in those places pluralism is taken for granted. Citizens of the southern region are either within the regional mainstream (which is rather wide) or they must locate their position with reference to it for both themselves and others.

3. "Born-again Christians" is a term which has a familiar ring down South but is apt to conjure up a spectacle of weird or obnoxious people in the North. There are of course, numbers there who so describe the nature of their Christian experience, but hearing the phrase "born-again" is jolting to northern sensibilities. Standard talk among the southern religious, "born-again" language nevertheless takes several different forms, all of them pointing toward a central claim: The believer underwent conversion in a datable, memorable experience; before that he was lost, from that moment on he is a saved person.

4. The recent evangelical resurgence in the United States is more notably a northern than a southern phenomenon. The North, comparatively free of such high-intensity, highly demonstrative forms, is more receptive to them. In the South, the presence of such forms has been standard for many decades, leaving less room for any variations on that theme. The principle at work would seem to be that progress from cold to hot is more likely than from warm to hot. In those sectors where this latest revival of religion is attractive to Southerners, its appeal is typically to members

of more formal churches who suddenly discover faith as heart-power and personal warmth, becoming assured and expressive.

5. Our final illustration pertains to the crises associated with the environment and energy which dominate today's news. As befits their respective theological and ethical traditions, we may expect the northern churches to be far more articulate and active on behalf of these causes than the southern. Concern for them will surely generate awareness and activity throughout the society. The southern religious are not likely to view these as directly Christian issues and responsibilities, however; that kind of reaction is far more predictable from the ranks of northern churchmen. The southern mentality is likely to treat them as matters of great human and social importance without seeing them as the proper province of the church, whose calling is in "spiritual" areas.

And so the distinction between South and North in American religion continues. Always limited because of so much shared history and unity in a single national society, the distinction is more difficult to perceive as the 1980s begin, because it is smaller. The notion that the South has an identity distinct from the rest of the national culture (the old "North") is without any real social significance in our times—cultural significance there may be, but social, virtually none. This is clearly demonstrated by the eroded social role of religion in the contemporary South. Diverse options in religious positioning are now attractive; one of these is the new freedom to be avowedly secularist. Candidates for public office are no longer under social pressure to flout religious convictions and activities.

The correlation between "ethos" and "ethic" endures as the major device for penetrating the southern and northern religious situations. Southern religion perpetuates its tradition of minding the churches' business instead of the society's. Under contemporary conditions that means that the churches still reflect and contribute to an identifiably southern culture, but also that their capacity for shaping a society has been blunted considerably. In other words, the religion characteristic of the North throughout this century has met its likeness in the South, in the course of that region's evolution. The religious life of the two regions is more similar and more closely related than it was in the colonial period. The wheel has come full circle, and even moved a few degrees beyond.

Notes

Introduction

1. Lewis P. Simpson, *The Dispossessed Garden* (Athens: University of Georgia Press, 1975), p. 15.
2. H. Richard Niebuhr, *Christ and Culture* (New York: Harper and Brothers, 1951).
3. Donald G. Mathews, *Religion in the Old South* (Chicago: University of Chicago Press, 1977), p. 249.

ONE—*First Cousins Separated, 1795–1810*

1. Carl N. Degler, *Place over Time* (Baton Rouge: Louisiana State University Press, 1976), pp. 32, 61–62, 90; Charles S. Sydnor, *The Development of Southern Sectionalism* (Baton Rouge: Louisiana State University Press, 1948), pp. 89, 102, 339.
2. Degler, *Place over Time*, pp. 31–32.
3. Carl Bridenbaugh, *Myths and Realities: Societies of the Colonial South* (Baton Rouge: Louisiana State University Press, 1952).
4. Rhys Isaac, "Evangelical Revolt: The Nature of the Baptists' Challenge to the Traditional Order in Virginia, 1765 to 1775," *William and Mary Quarterly* 31 (July 1974): 368.
5. Albert J. Raboteau, *Slave Religion* (New York: Oxford University Press, 1978), pp. 125–26.
6. Ibid., pp. 126–27.
7. Ibid., p. 128, quoting Frank J. Klingberg.
8. Raboteau, *Slave Religion*, pp. 132–33.
9. Mathews, *Religion in the Old South*, p. 50.
10. William G. McLoughlin, *Revivals, Awakenings, and Reform* (Chicago: University of Chicago Press, 1978), p. 132.
11. Mathews, *Religion in the Old South*, p. 40.
12. Ibid., pp. 37–38.
13. McLoughlin, *Revivals*, p. 137.

14. A full-scale treatment of the relation between the outlooks of these religious bodies and the political spirit of the age is found in Nathan O. Hatch, "The Christian Movement and the Demand for a Theology of the People," an unpublished paper cited by permission of the author.

15. Edmund S. Morgan, "The American Revolution Considered as an Intellectual Movement" in *Paths of American Thought*, ed. Arthur M. Schlesinger, Jr., and Morton White (Boston: Houghton Mifflin Co., 1963) , pp. 11–33.

16. McLoughlin, *Revivals*, pp. 107, 109.

17. Bernard Bailyn et al., *The Great Republic* (Boston: Little, Brown and Company, 1977) , p. 507.

18. McLoughlin, *Revivals*, p. 137.

TWO—*Third Cousins Alienated, 1835–1850*

1. C. Vann Woodward, *American Counterpoint* (Boston: Little, Brown and Company, 1971) , p. 11.

2. Degler, *Place over Time*, pp. 33, 36, 60.

3. Quoted in Clement Eaton, *The Leaven of Democracy* (New York: G. Braziller, 1963) , p. 16.

4. Ibid.

5. Bailyn et al., *The Great Republic*, p. 566.

6. Ibid., p. 567.

7 Sydnor, *Southern Sectionalism*, pp. 2, 32.

8. Robert N. Bellah, "Transcendence in Contemporary Culture," in *Transcendence*, ed. Herbert W. Richardson and Donald R. Cutler (Boston: Beacon Press, 1969) , p. 91.

9. Degler, *Place over Time*, p. 90.

10. Ibid., pp. 76, 81.

11. Clement Eaton, *The Growth of Southern Civilization* (New York: Harper, 1961), p. 314.

12. Clement Eaton, *The Waning of the Old South Civilization* (Athens: University of Georgia Press, 1968) , p. 22.

13. Sydnor, *Southern Sectionalism*, p. 294.

14. Eaton, *The Leaven of Democracy*, p. 17.

15. Stanley M. Elkins, *Slavery* (Chicago: University of Chicago Press, 1959) , pp. 60–61.

16. Ibid.

17. Elkins, *Slavery*, p. 61.

18. Donald G. Mathews, *Slavery and Methodism* (Princeton: Princeton University Press, 1965) , p. 62.

19. Raboteau, *Slave Religion*, p. 174.

20. Mathews, *Slavery and Methodism*, p. 62.

21. Ibid., p. 70.

22. Raboteau, *Slave Religion*, pp. 161–62.

23. Charles Grier Sellers, *The Southerner as American* (Chapel Hill: University of North Carolina Press, 1960), pp. 40–71.

24. John Hope Franklin, *An American Odyssey* (Baton Rouge: Louisiana State University Press, 1976), passim.

25. Fletcher M. Green, *The Role of the Yankee in the Old South* (Athens: University of Georgia Press, 1972), ch. 4.

26. Mathews, *Slavery and Methodism*, ch. 9.

27. Ibid., p. 281.

28. Raboteau, *Slave Religion*, p. 157.

29. Ibid., p. 158.

30. Ibid., p. 160.

31. Ibid., p. 157.

32. Degler, *Place over Time*, p. 32.

33. Ibid., p. 93.

34. Ibid., pp. 61–62.

35. Sydnor, *Southern Sectionalism*, pp. 88, 89, ch. 15.

36. Woodward, *American Counterpoint*, p. 154.

37. Quoted in ibid., p. 157.

38. Quoted in ibid., p. 146.

39. David M. Potter, *The Impending Crisis 1848–1861* (New York: Harper and Row, 1976), p. 472.

40. Jon Alexander, "A Drift toward Disparity: The Religious Experiences of Southerners and Northerners in the Antebellum Period," an unpublished paper used by permission.

41. Mathews, *Religion in the Old South*, p. 38.

42. Howard Becker, "Sacred and Secular Societies," *Social Forces* 28 (May, 1950): 361–76.

43. Avery Craven, *An Historian and the Civil War* (Chicago: University of Chicago Press, 1964), pp. 215–16.

44. E. Brooks Holifield, *The Gentlemen Theologians* (Durham, N.C.: Duke University Press, 1978), p. 27.

45. Ibid., pp. 3, 4.

46. Ibid., p. 154.

47. Ibid., p. 197.

48. Emory M. Thomas, *The Confederate Nation* (New York: Harper and Row, 1979), p. 21.

THREE—*Strangers in the Same Household, 1885–1900*

1. C. Vann Woodward, *Origins of the New South* (Baton Rouge: Louisiana State University Press, 1951), p. 450.

2. Potter, *Impending Crisis*, p. 469.

3. See Charles Reagan Wilson, *Baptized in Blood: The Religion of the Lost Cause, 1865–1920* (Athens: University of Georgia Press, 1980).

4. Eaton, *Waning of the Old South*, p. 171.

5. Quoted in ibid., p. 166.

6. Robert H. Wiebe, *The Search for Order* (New York: Hill and Wang, 1963), ch. 2.

7. Woodward, *Origins of the New South*, pp. 110–11.

8. Quoted in ibid., p. 140.

9. Ibid., p. 354.

10. Raboteau, *Slave Religion*, pp. 266–71.

11. Kenneth K. Bailey, *Southern White Protestantism in the Twentieth Century* (New York: Harper, 1964), p. 6.

12. Hunter Dickinson Farish, *The Circuit Rider Dismounts* (Richmond: The Dietz Press, 1938), p. 82.

13. Ibid., p. 83, and Raboteau, *Slave Religion*, p. 175.

14. Bailey, *Southern White Protestantism*, p. 4.

15. See Mathews, *Religion in the Old South*, p. 186.

16. John Lee Eighmy, *Churches in Cultural Captivity* (Knoxville: University of Tennessee Press, 1972), p. 30.

17. Ibid., pp. 37, 38.

18. Robert A. Baker, *The Southern Baptist Convention and Its People* (Nashville: Broadman Press, 1974), pp. 359, 260.

19. Ibid., p. 316.

20. Paul H. Buck, *Road to Reunion* (Boston: Little, Brown, and Company, 1937), p. 60.

21. Bailey, *Southern White Protestantism*, p. 24.

22. See ibid., ch. 1.

23. Buck, *Road to Reunion*, p. 305.

24. Irwin T. Hyatt, *Their Ordered Lives Confess* (Cambridge: Harvard University Press, 1976), pp. 133, 134.

25. Farish, *The Circuit Rider Dismounts*, p. 105.

26. Woodward, *Origins of the New South*, p. 448.

27. Charles A. Scarboro, ".A Sectarian Religious Organization in Heterogeneous Society: The Churches of Christ and the Plain-Folk of the Transmontane South," Ph.D. dissertation, Emory University, 1976, p. 8.

28. Bailey, *Southern White Protestantism*, p. 16.

29. Eighmy, *Churches in Cultural Captivity*, p. 75.

30. Degler, *Place over Time*, p. 8.

31. William G. McLoughlin, *Modern Revivalism* (New York: Ronald Press, 1959), p. 291.

32. Farish, *The Circuit Rider Dismounts*, p. 303.

33. McLoughlin, *Revivals*, p. 136.

34. Quoted in Ernest Trice Thompson, *Presbyterians in the South* (Richmond: John Knox Press, 1973), 2:403.

35. Quoted in Buck, *Road to Reunion*, p. 59.

36. See Martin E. Marty, *Righteous Empire* (New York: Dial Press, 1970), ch. 17.

37. Joseph R. Gusfield, *Symbolic Crusade* (Urbana: University of Illinois Press, 1963), pp. 3–4.

38. See Rowland T. Berthoff, "Southern Attitudes toward Immigration," *Journal of Southern History* 12 (August 1951) : 328–60.

39. Eighmy, *Churches in Cultural Captivity*, pp. 52–54.

40. Thompson, *Presbyterians in the South*, pp. 402–3.

41. Farish, *The Circuit Rider Dismounts*, p. 320.

42. John R. Earle, Dean D. Knudsen, and Donald W. Shriver, *Spindles and Spires* (Atlanta: John Knox Press, 1975), p. 305.

Index

60, 80–81, 115, public higher, 65;
its liberalizing impact, 123–24. *See
also* Biblical criticism
Eighmy, John L., xii, 102, 114
Elkins, Stanley M., 53, 55
Episcopal Church, 17, 51. *See also*
Church of England
Epoch A (1795–1810), xv, 9, 11–12,
13–45, 46–47, 91, 136–37
Epoch B (1835–1850), xv, 9, 12, 14,
45, 46–89, 91, 136–37
Epoch C (1885–1900), ix, 9, 12, 14,
59, 73, 90–135, 136–37
Ethical responsibility, 2, 3, 4, 7, 8,
11, 30–31, 32, 35. *See also* "Ethos
and ethic," "Spirituality of the
church"
"Ethos and ethic," 6–7, 8, 35, 74–
75, 83, 88, 140–41. *See also* Ethical responsibility
European religion, 1, 4, 5, 10, 59
Evangelicalism, xi, 3, 22, 24–25, 42,
70, 71–73, 86–87, 120–21, 139–40;
northern, 4, 38, 71–73; social impact of, 7, 26–28, 42, 75; theology
of, 22–23, 37–38, 43, 73; individualism in, 38, 88–89; southern
hegemony of, xi, 2, 52, 70, 72,
125–26, 139
Evangelization: of the South, 5, 42,
44, 70–71, 121–22; of the North,
5, 34, 70–71, 121
Ewing, Finis, 32

Farish, Hunter D., xii, 109–10, 125
Fiedler, Leslie, 108
Finney, Charles G., 121, 123
Foreign missionary enterprise, 107–9
Franklin, John Hope, xiii, 14, 59
Frontier religion, 21–22, 23, 36, 43,
106

Gentlemen Theologians, The, 80–
83
German Protestantism, 20
Great Awakenings, 11, 17, 21, 27,
29–30, 39, 44, 121, 122, 127
Great Republic, The, 93
Green, Fletcher M., xiii, 61
Gusfield, Joseph R., xiii, 131

Haygood, Atticus G., 110
Helper, Hinton R., 51
Holifield, E. Brooks, xi, xii, 80–83
Holiness movement, 32, 138
Holy Commonwealth, North as, 4,
10, 34–35, 36, 127
Hyatt, Irwin T., 107–9

Immigration and immigrants, 59,
76–77, 93, 106, 132; and South, 79,
132
Indigenous religious movements: in
South, 31–33, 42–43, 69, 111; in
North, 69–70
Isaac, Rhys, 9–10, 18

Jews, 1, 2, 76, 118–19; in South, 20,
79
Jim Crow era, 91, 96, 105
Jones, Charles Colcock, 58, 64, 66
Jones, Sam P., 121

Ku Klux Klan, 78

Landmarkism, 114
Liberal religion, 39, 40, 44, 72, 81,
82–83, 85
"Lost Cause, The," 91, 92

McLoughlin, William G., 21, 27,
29–30, 39, 44, 45, 121, 127
Marty, Martin E., xii
Mathews, Donald G., xi, xii, 7, 16,
24, 27, 28, 55, 56, 63, 75
Methodist church, 3, 16, 17, 20–21,
24, 36, 39, 40, 51, 57, 62, 101, 102,
103, 125, 133; Wesleyan Methodist
Church, 32; Methodist Episcopal
Church, South, 56–57, 62, 69, 99,
128, 133; African Methodist Epis-
copal Church, 98; African Metho-
dist Episcopal, Zion, Church, 98–
99; Colored Methodist Episcopal
Church, 99. *See also* Negroes
Migration, westward, 14, 21, 36
Mission to the Slaves, 53, 56
Miyakawa, T. Scott, 42
Modernization, process of, 10–11,
76, 94, 122, 134
Moody, Dwight L., 121